PHOTOGRAPHER'S GUIDE TO NEW ENGLAND

A YANKEE BOOKS TRAVEL GUIDE

PHOTOGRAPHER'S GUIDE TO NEW ENGLAND

by Gordon A. Reims

YANKEE BOOKS

Camden, Maine

Text Design • Amy Fischer, Camden, Maine
Cover Design • Dale Swensson, Mt. Desert, Maine
Composition • High Resolution, Inc., Camden, Maine

Printed in the United States

Library of Congress Cataloging-in-Publication Data

Reims, Gordon A., 1918-
    Photographer's guide to New England / by Gordon A. Reims.
        p.   cm. — (A Yankee Books travel guide)
    ISBN 0-89909-328-0
    1. New England—Description and travel—1981- —Guide-books.
    2. Photography—New England—Guide-books. I. Title. II. Series.
    F2.3.R45   1991
    917.404'43—dc20   91-13462
                                                                  CIP

10 9 8 7 6 5 4 3 2 1

CONTENTS

INTRODUCTION

A few years ago, when doing photographic work in midcoast Maine, I was often asked by visitors where to obtain good shots of such things as lobster boats or colonial houses, or perhaps a particular lighthouse they had seen on a book jacket. One man even asked, "Where's the ocean?" He'd come to the Maine coast seeking to photograph ocean breakers surging on granite shores, but every seacoast town he visited proved to be on a peaceful bay with protective islands offshore.

I can sympathize with perplexities of this kind, as I've encountered similar situations while touring various parts of the country. In fact, I'm one of those people who can't look at a television car commercial with a mountain or city skyline in the background without trying to figure out where the shots were taken. Geographical identification, unfortunately, is seldom provided. This is true of many a published New England scene. The prime covered bridges, lighthouses, or village greens we've all seen so often

GREENVALE COVE, RANGELEY LAKE, RANGELEY, MAINE.

*New England . . .
a region
seemingly
designed with
photographers
in mind.*

on calendars or in pictorial guides are rarely captioned as to location, and the stranger seeking them to take similar pictures can wind up on many a false trail.

Sure, if you're visiting Vermont and want to photograph Mount Mansfield or Queechee Gorge or the Coolidge home, you can find them easily on the maps. But if you're seeking a truly photogenic covered bridge, a spectacular waterfall, or that particular white steepled-village you've seen pictured many times, location unidentified, you might drive within a mile of each and not know it.

Realizing all of this, I felt that a photographer's guide — a "where to" — for New England would be appreciated; perhaps a guide of specific use to photographers, but at the same time broad enough in scope to be of some use to the entire family.

In planning this guide we quickly encountered a key question: would the reader prefer a chapter for each New England state, or a chapter for each season of the year? We elected to do it both ways. Each seasonal chapter suggests what you can best see or do photographically at that time of year, with a number of key examples, such as waterfalls and covered bridges in summer and public gardens in spring. The autumn chapter obviously centers on autumn foliage, and in it we've tried to answer as many questions as possible as to when and where to find fall colors at their best, including a few specific locations and back roads where we've had autumn foliage success at one time or another. The winter chapter concentrates on photography at ski areas and other winter sports possibilities, touching as well on the potentials of the snow-covered countryside.

In the remaining chapters we zero in on each state, spotlighting specific local points of photographic interest, such as a dominant cliff-top lighthouse, a striking statue, or a tall church tower on a tidy village green. We don't claim to know every nook and corner of New England, but we have wandered with camera into a lot of places, made a few discoveries, and enjoy "talking" about them. We're sure you'll discover your own gems — New England makes it easy for you.

Other sections of the country may be rich in photographic scenes, particularly the western states with their broad sweeps of scenic grandeur. But I know of no region with so thorough a mixture of photogenic subjects within so comparatively small a territory as New England. It's a region seemingly designed with photographers in mind — where old schooners, steep waterfalls, red covered bridges, city skylines, rustic village greens, soaring mountains, lonely lighthouses, stacked lobster traps, and colonial church towers are all placed about as though awaiting the camera, some hidden like eggs in an Easter egg hunt, others as conspicuous as an eagle over the mantlepiece.

Because the region is so compact, no six states anywhere else can be toured as rapidly, and therefore as inexpensively, as the states of New England. You can awaken in your motel in Kittery, Maine, and have your breakfast two states away in Massachusetts, just a 20-mile drive across the intervening coastal section of New Hampshire. Then, you might circle Boston on I-95, take Route 24 southward through Taunton and Fall River, and enjoy your lunch in Newport, Rhode Island. Even if you spent much of the afternoon sightseeing and taking pictures in Newport, you could easily make it to a Connecticut motel for the night. (In the trip I'm thinking of, we made it all the way to Danbury.) We don't advise that you always travel so hurriedly; we just wish to illustrate how the nearness of photographic scenes to each other in New England can keep your photo appetite whetted and your camera clicking.

Everyone has his or her own photographic preferences. Perhaps some of you are not interested in pointing cameras at state capitols or city skylines, but at such things as ivy entwining a fencepost, spring flowers bending over a brook sparkling in the sun, or a child petting a cow through a break in a rustic fence. So in addition to pointing out specific landmarks or natural splendors, we've made an effort to reveal the type of countryside, mood, and atmosphere encountered in various regions of the six states. Those who shoot with videotape should be helped here too, as we've covered many a scene and event where action is at hand — waterfalls, rapids, boat races, ocean surf, county fairs, and the like.

What we don't want to do is "sell" readers on any particular location or type of subject. We're just letting you know what's out there. You do the rest, in accordance with your own preferences and inclinations.

We've made an effort to reveal the type of countryside, mood, and atmosphere encountered in various regions of the six states.

PHOTOGRAPHER'S GUIDE TO NEW ENGLAND

SUMMER

Summer photography in New England can mean
shots of the wild and craggy spires of rock that
soar skyward above the parking field at Franconia
Notch, in New Hampshire, or an angle shot of the
magnificent church tower on Litchfield's immaculate
green in Connecticut, or a close-up of the reaching
bowsprit of a Camden or Rockland schooner on the
Maine coast. Cameras may point at a group of cows
grazing in a meadow at the edge of a winding
Vermont stream, or at one of those magnificent time-
worn colonial doorways in Deerfield, Massachusetts,
or at a grinning child, blueberry pie in hand, emerging from the food tent at Union, Maine's Blueberry
Festival. They may even point at the build-up of a
dramatic thunderhead above the steeples and gables
of Lancaster, New Hampshire, or at Atlantic breakers
crashing below Cliff Walk in Rhode Island.

Summer is a great time in New England. Days are

SMALL'S FALLS, MADRID, MAINE.

warm; everything in nature that is supposed to be green is green; beaches and parks are open; festivals and other outdoor activities are in full swing; and light is strong and long for the taking of pictures. Except for the lack of snow, ice, and autumn foliage, there is very little you can't do photographically in summer.

If you'd like a word on the weather, it's not very different from summer weather elsewhere, if you'll just allow the coastal edge north of Boston to warm up a bit later in the season that the inland areas. It makes up for it by prolonging the summer in September, often with sunny, tranquil days of the type that lead people to say, "This is the way I wish it would be all year long."

"This is the way I wish it would be all year long."

The Connecticut River valley is usually the warmest area in New England, with temperatures of 90° no stranger to Hartford in July or August. The mountain areas northward are, of course, usually much cooler and experience quick drops in temperature at night, even in the warmest of weather. The upper trails and summits in the White Mountains will likely oblige sweaters at any time of summer.

Although mountain areas in the northern portions may be prone to sudden showers at times, rain is seldom a summer problem in New England. Rain in warm weather ususally comes in the evening or during the night, occasionally in thunderstorm activity. Quite a few entertaining "boomers" roll into the Berkshires at night from the Hudson River valley, and the Green Mountains in Vermont are good producers of electrical storms — for those who want to stand the camera on a tripod and leave the shutter open to record lightning flashes.

Where the scene aspect is concerned, there is a varied array across the six states. Much of Vermont, New Hampshire, and Maine offer forested mountains. New Hampshire's high and dramatically rugged, Maine's more distinguished by wilderness, and Vermont's more shadily foliaged and gently contoured. Let's say you will expect to meet a hiker in the New Hampshire woods; a bear in the forests of Maine; and if you have a reasonable imagination, an elf, gnome, or leprechaun in the wooded slopes of Vermont. (Unfortunately, the latter three characters won't register on even the best of films!)

To the south, the Connecticut River Valley, the Berkshires, and the gently rolling hills of Connecticut present their soft panoramas of colonial villages, meadowed countryside, and historic sites. Here are the prime village greens, the just-right campuses, the venerable church towers, and that clean white-against-green New England rural look so often captured on film.

The coastal areas present New England's colorful marine aspect. The lobstering coves of Maine; the small harbors with cruise schooners readying to sail; the sun dancing on blue waters dotted with white sails at the start of a regatta, and of course, surf crashing on rocks or sand and sentinel lighthouses atop bluffs or cliffs. Small excursion boats that leave bright foamy wakes take you to coastal islands or across city harbors. The sun dazzles on Cape Cod beaches and dunes, or on those intriguing little paths between spreads of dune grass, where you squint through your finder at windmills or weather-beaten cottages. At the various county fairs, prize cattle stand blissfully in their stalls, the ferris wheels turn, and children squeal on exciting rides.

Waterfalls

Perhaps one of the favorite summer targets of photographers is the waterfall.

PERHAPS ONE of the favorite summer targets of photographers — and not necessarily identified with any particular New England state — is the waterfall. In early summer, waterfalls are generally close to their peak in water volume, and the trails that lead to them have shed the muddiness of spring that might have made them a bit difficult earlier on.

The most photogenic waterfalls in the White Mountains of New Hampshire are probably Glen Ellis Falls, just off Route 16, and Arethusa Falls, high in the forest off Route 302. Glen Ellis Falls, more frequently visited, is in a state park with its own parking field, which can be entered directly from Route 16 a few miles north of Glen and just south of Glen House. Wide paths take you quickly and easily to the falls, which gush lustily over a steep cliff into a rocky pool and gorge. You can photograph the falls from above or below, and the rapids above are interesting in themselves.

Arethusa Falls is not located in a maintained park in the same sense as Glen Ellis Falls, although it is within the borders of the extensive Crawford Notch State Park. It is in a thoroughly unspoiled forest location, 700 feet above Route 302 and about one and one-half miles along a winding, climbing trail. If you don't mind a hike of this kind, by all means take the time to see it. The path is not too steep, and although there might be one or two rough spots where small brooks cross, you don't have to be a rugged out-

ARETHUSA FALLS, CRAWFORD
NOTCH STATE PARK,
NEW HAMPSHIRE.

doorsman to make the trek. Nearly 100 feet high, Arethusa rarely fails to startle newcomers, particularly because you'll first see its curving crest above the treetops as you approach. It is a magnificently photogenic waterfall, and you'll be tempted to use up much film shooting from various angles.

The Arethusa Falls turn-off is on Route 302 about three miles south of Willey House and is clearly labeled. The trail into the woods from the small parking area is well marked, and in fact becomes an access to the Appalachian Trail. Continuing beyond Arethusa Falls, a branch of this trail will take you to the summit of Frankenstein Cliffs, a favorite spot for hikers and a fine vantage point for views of Crawford Notch.

There are other waterfalls in Crawford Notch, notably Ripley Falls, which is similar to Arethusa but somewhat smaller and less striking. The trail to Ripley, a bit shorter than the Arethusa trail, is also marked by a sign on Route 302, a bend or two up the road north of the Arethusa trail.

At the northern end of Crawford Notch, where Route 302 climbs steadily toward the actual notch, or cleft, in the mountain barrier, is beautiful Silver Cascades, which you can view or photograph while standing at the edge of the road. Just a slender rivulet, it comes glistening and ribboning toward you from hundreds of feet above. It's tough to photograph well, but give it a try!

If you approach the Rangeley Lakes from the south on Route 4 in Maine, you might easily drive within 200 yards of a magnificent multitiered waterfall without realizing it, so hidden is it from sight by roadside foliage. It is regularly missed by countless tourists. A generous surprise is granted those who heed an inconspicuous sign just a bit north of the village of Madrid, reading "Picnic Area 2 Miles."

The picnic area is there all right, and if you don't have to watch traffic too closely, you'll notice the words "Smalls Falls" on the turn-off sign. Turning in, you'll find the picnic area agreeably spacious, with a large parking field and paths leading to the shore of a wide stream. Upon reaching the shore, you'll behold a magnificent triple-tiered waterfall roaring down at you between steep granite cliffs like something out of the Far West. This is the youthful Sandy River, plunging from ledge to ledge for a total drop of 90 feet.

There is a footbridge across the small river, and paths lead up to the foot of the falls, where a broad, clear pool often attracts young waders. Here you'll discover an uppermost fourth tier of falls, not previously visible. Trails that are rough but not difficult lead all the way to the top of the fourth tier.

The falls are a delight to photographers, as the many natural vantage points afford varied and unimpeded views of tumbling water. Those with firm feet may find any number of dizzying angle shots. The course of the stream is wide enough to admit ample light, and in the late morning or at noon, the entire length of the falls dazzles in sunlight.

Each of the four tiers of the falls is a respectable waterfall in its own right, and the tall bordering cedars add to the scenic qualities. At the base of the falls, a large, reddish, inward-curving cliff forms a dramatic backdrop for the swirling pool. The falls have a number of regular visitors. We met one octogenarian on the rocks at the fourth tier who told us that he has climbed to the top every year since boyhood. (And we don't think he ever bothered to stop and picnic!)

Into the woods, farther from the highway, you can cross a low knoll and encounter Chandler Mill Falls. This would likely prove a scenic attraction itself were the larger Smalls Falls not close by. Chandler Mill Stream is smaller than the Sandy River, with which it shortly joins, but it tumbles over the same escarpment.

In the mountains south of Umbagog Lake, there's a wild and interesting set of rapids, known as Screw Auger Falls, carved into a rocky landscape at Grafton Notch. Route 26, which slants between Newry, Maine, and Errol, New Hampshire, passes Screw Auger Falls in a wildly beautiful countryside of open land with fine mountain views. The stream here curves and zigzags through miniature rocky canyons, falls across great tilted slabs of rock, and in general, creates some interesting water effects. There is ample parking at the site.

Vermont certainly has its share of good waterfalls. Two strong, picturesque ones that are only a few miles apart in the central portion of the state are particularly worth mentioning. Moss Glen Falls, immediately visible on the west side of Route 100, just eight miles south of Warren, is a broad, foamy waterfall that you can easily capture with a camera. There's also Texas Falls, which is a little more hidden and not as heavily signposted. To reach Texas Falls, turn west on Route 125 from Route 100, 10 miles south of Moss Glen Falls. About two or three miles along Route 125, you'll see the sign at the falls entrance. Nearby in the woods, Texas Falls is more rugged-based and wilder than Moss Glen Falls, but there are more railings and walkways in the area surrounding it.

The other New England states are by no means without their share of waterfalls, although those in the northern mountains may admittedly be the high-

Vermont certainly has its share of good waterfalls.

est. At Campbell Falls, the Bershires provide a comparatively light but lively cascade. Both Connecticut and Massachusetts maintain parks here, as the falls are almost exactly on the state line. The most direct way to reach Campbell Falls is to take Route 272 north from Norfolk on Route 44 in Connecticut.

Perhaps Connecticut's most attractive falls — and of the type that can be made quite poetic in appearance under certain light and treatment — are at Kent. Just north of New Milford on Route 7, Kent Falls has a roomy, broad-lawned state park built around it.

Covered Bridges

WE KNOW OF some photographers who wend their way into New England specifically to seek out covered bridges. Many return with beautiful shots, but a few find the bridges elusive, at least the better ones that they've seen on calendars and in coffee table books. Unfortunately, every little covered bridge symbol imprinted on a road map does not mean the presence of a picturesque gem. At last count there were at least 75 remaining covered bridges in New Hampshire alone, and probably an equal number in Vermont. Most are flagged on road maps, and if you visit state tourist information centers, you can often obtain listings of them. But I've never seen a list that differentiated between nonphotogenic bridges and pictorial beauties.

Far from all of these bridges have that just-right combination of well-maintained construction, red coloring, and green foliage background. Many not only lack the desired red color, but have lost whatever paint they once had. Others have obvious structural defects — they are losing their boards or a section of roof. A few, once included on lists or indicated on maps, may no longer be there at all. Whenever there are flooding rains of severe intensity, one or two covered bridges are damaged by swollen streams and not repaired. In those communities in which local historical societies can pass a big enough hat, you will usually see beautifully maintained covered bridges. A few lucky bridges are under the care and jurisdiction of state and local highway departments.

Finding a nice red covered bridge in decent repair does not ensure that you'll have a "cover picture" for the snapping. The views of great many covered bridges are blocked or marred by commercial structures, gravel banks, or perhaps heavy cables spanning the stream. Some have backgrounds that do not

Some photographers wend their way into New England specifically to seek out covered bridges.

A COVERED BRIDGE AT WEST SWANZEY, NEW HAMPSHIRE.

do the bridge justice, or that break the "mood" of a tranquil old-fashioned scene. And even some of the best ones, with nothing but green foliage at each end, can be difficult to photograph well. Heavy trees can block your view, or steep banks that are difficult to cling to may prevent you from shooting from what seems the best vantage point. The only spot from which to get a really good picture might also be on someone's private fenced-in lawn.

But don't let us discourage you — there are still plenty of covered bridges we find no fault with. Quite possibly the top gem among New England covered bridges is the first one encountered as you cross the state line from New York into Connecticut. It spans the Housatonic River in Connecticut at West Cornwall, just 25 miles north of New Milford, on Route 7. Many other bridges in New England are longer, cross wider rivers, or have more spectacular natural scenery behind them, but for an exceptionally well-maintained red bridge in a tranquil, unspoiled setting that is easy to photograph, you can't beat this one.

A handful of white houses are gathered at the eastern end of the bridge, the western shore is thickly wooded, and there are no unsightly structures or other objects to mar the river scene upstream or downstream from it. Even Route 7, following the western shore of the river, is hidden in foliage. A wooden railing at a little walk-to spot immediately upriver from the bridge entrance on the village side provides an excellent camera vantage point. The bridge, smoothly red, can be viewed in its entirety from here across the slowly swirling waters, framed nicely under arched branches.

There are covered bridges in all sections of New England, but most are in New Hampshire and Vermont. We recommend one specific area in New Hampshire where more well-maintained and highly photographable covered bridges can be found within a few miles of each other than anywhere else in the state. This is the area along and between Routes 10 and 32, from the Massachusetts line to Keene. There are several bridges in this vicinity, including two at Swanzey, that offer fine photogenic viewpoints and are usually maintained in good appearance. The local communities are proud of these bridges, and road intersection signs call attention to most of them.

The White Mountains area of New Hampshire, although not as famous for covered bridges as the lower part of the state, is not without a fine example. You'll find a hefty covered bridge in a rugged mountain setting at Jackson, just off Route 16 north of North Conway.

Vermont's sprawling farm areas have many an old covered bridge tucked away on back roads as they lead away from village centers. Many of them are not visible until you come upon them, as the streams they cross are often in leafy dips and valleys. A good way to locate them is to follow the river and stream lines on your map. You're likely to find a bridge wherever your road encounters a fairsized town on a broad stream. If the road parallels the stream, check village side streets for crossing points. At Montgomery, near Vermont's Canadian border east of Enosburg Falls, there are six covered bridges within a radius of five miles. Vermont's often-mentioned railroad covered bridge is visible across a broad field from Route 15 between the villages of Hardwick and Wolcott, and as of recently, was still nicely painted and accessible by path.

At Windsor, Vermont, the longest covered bridge in New England crosses the Connecticut River to Cornish Mills, New Hampshire. Althought this bridge is not a colorful red at this writing (it once was), and it crosses perhaps too much water to give a peaceful, old backcountry mood picture, its sheer length makes it a bridge you'll likely want to photograph. The best view of the bridge is, we believe, from Route 12A on

There are covered bridges in all sections of New England, but most are in New Hampshire and Vermont.

the New Hampshire side, about a half-mile northward. This viewpoint enables you to capture the entire length of the bridge and both shores, with the lofty mass of Mount Ascutney rising picturesquely in the background. The state of New Hampshire, which owns the bridge, has created a scenic parking spot at the immediate end of the bridge, but while this vantage point is great for a close look, you can't photograph the entire bridge from here without a wideangle lens.

One of the most photogenic covered bridges in Massachusetts is the Bissel Bridge at Charlemont, in the eastern foothills of the Berkshires, on Route 2. This well cared for bridge crosses a deep river ravine, and although it takes a bit of rock and bramble scrambling to capture the full bridge with the waters beneath it, the handsome entrance to the bridge makes a nice head-on shot.

Although there are not as many covered bridges in Maine as in Vermont and New Hampshire, a particularly attractive Maine bridge may be found at Newry, on Route 2, about 15 miles east of the New Hampshire state line.

When photographing covered bridges, you are likely to get the most pleasing results if you shoot the bridge from across the water, show it in its entirety (preferably at an angle from one of the shores, not head-on), and show the opening at one end. Hopefully, the bridge will be red and you will be able to photograph the sunny side. A couple of people or a boy and his dog, perhaps seated on the bank at one end of the bridge, would add a nice touch — but you can't always have everything.

Sunsets

ONE OF SUMMER's better attributes, as far as the photographer is concerned, is its long days. Strong sunshine lasts until well into evening, and twilight a fair bit beyond that. If you don't want to hole up in your motel after supper and settle down before a television set, there's a top photogenic world out there at sundown. Sunsets are glorious climaxes for picture-taking days. They're at their best over lakes and harbors, not merely because expanses of water are interesting, but also because they're much brighter than any land foreground. We suggest you scout potential locations earlier in the day — if you know for sure, that is, approximately where the sun will go down.

One of summer's better attributes is its long days.

Try to select a point where you look across water at a hill or mountain, or where there is something interesting in the foreground, such as a moored sloop or even just a bit of rustic fence with an arching tree branch overhead. Sunsets over Lake Champlain from the Vermont shore have been highly praised, but because the lake expanse is so great, a good photo requires care and planning — include a large ferry, pier, or shore building in the foreground and use a telephoto lens if you want to take advantage of the distant Adirondack Mountains as background. Sunset over mountains with lake in the foreground can be captured to fine advantage from a boat in most any of Maine's Rangeley Lakes.

It should perhaps be noted here that a sunrise is usually indistinguishable from a sunset in a photo. Although you can't very well get a sunset shot in New England with tumbling ocean surf in the foreground, a sunrise shot would do just as well. You need to be an early riser, particularly in June or July, but rising suns, casting orange trails across breaking surf, can be caught on the Maine or New Hampshire coasts as well as at Cape Cod and a few headlands in

A RANGELEY LAKE BEAUTIFUL SUNSET, RANGELEY, MAINE.

between. Late summer will likely provide more clear mornings than early summer.

Returning to the day's close, city skylines are at their best at dusk, when lights are on in the buildings and the skies beyond them remain reasonably bright. You want the lights to be bright enough to show, but you also want enough daylight at hand to fill in shadowy sections just a bit. In both sunset shots and city twilight views, exposures can be tricky. If you shoot for prints rather than slides, the results may disappoint you, as computer controlled printing operations will automatically try to brighten the areas you want dark and, in the process, will wash out delicate sunset sky effects. Meters can fool you in these situations too, as they tend to over-respond to the setting sun and to the bright sky behind window-lit skyscrapers.

With sunsets, especially when the sun is a red ball about to go under, lean toward a slower exposure than your meter or your mental calculations dictate. Everything other than the sun itself is darker than you think at that time. I've found that I've underexposed more often than I've overexposed in these situations.

When tackling a sunset do take more than one shot, trying various exposures. But you'll have to work fast when the sun gets close to the horizon — it sinks pretty rapidly, and the overall light in the sky and on the water dwindles quickly in the final minute.

AUTUMN

Nowhere in the world are the hues more rich and varied than in the climax woodlands of the eastern United States" wrote Edwin Way Teale in *Autumn Across America*. World travelers have often expressed surprise at the brilliance of color in the American northeast, and as Massachusetts' own Henry David Thoreau once said of the New England sugar maple, "As I look up Main Street, they appear like painted screens standing before the houses. . . . all the sunny warmth of the season, the Indian summer, seems to be absorbed in their leaves."

Since Thoreau's day, people have been journeying to view New England's autumn foliage in ever-increasing numbers. The special attraction of fall foliage here is perhaps due to the high percentage of maples and other brilliant display trees, plus the fact that cooling weather strikes these trees earlier in their yearly cycle than in regions farther south. The pattern of the New England countryside is also ideal for autumn color, with foliage thrust upward on hill and mountain slopes for greater visibility, and numerous photogenic barns, meadows, and church steeples on hand to enhance the view.

A broad stream where brilliant gold boughs bend close over the water; a wide meadow where tall flaming orange trees stand close to a red barn; or a main street of old white houses with yellow Norway maples shedding their leaves on gateposts and slate paths — all are typical aspects of autumn New England.

Beautiful shots can be taken on at least three levels — broad, sweeping panoramas, shorter views of colorful village greens or barnyards, and close-ups of bright branches bending over mailboxes or fieldstone walls. Very striking pictures may even be taken of individual leaves themselves; perhaps a group of two or three on the weathered stones of a bridge, or drifting in a quiet stream.

The color peak usually takes about a month to move across New England.

As summer ends in New England, trees in mountain areas farthest from the sea usually turn first, and color appears initially in the mountains of northern Vermont. From there the color advances eastward and southward, touching Cape Cod and the Rhode Island shore last. The color peak usually takes about a month to move across New England, beginning in late September and ending in late October. City foliage is slow to turn and doesn't give the finest of displays, simply because cities are warmer than the open country around them, particularly at night. Some trees in Boston Common are often still green on November first. Seashore towns also tend toward later autumn foliage, because the ocean is still summer warm in October, and sea breezes can help keep nights from becoming too cool.

The Best Autumn Foliage

THERE IS GOOD foliage just about anywhere in New England, and we can point out some particularly good spots in each of the states. But if you want to center your visit on one general area with the greatest likely concentration of foliageviewing opportunities, we have to recommend either the area within a 50-mile radius of Brattleboro, Vermont (including part of New Hampshire and the Berkshires), or the Connecticut River Valley between the White Mountains and the Green Mountains.

The greatest concentrations of people viewing

foliage are likely in the Berkshires, the Brattleboro area of Vermont, and the southwest corner of New Hampshire. Should you plan to visit these areas during autumn foliage time, be sure to have motel reservations in advance, as the concentration of visitors is greater then than in July. You'll also find large numbers of travelers visiting the Route 7 towns north into the Arlington-Manchester region of Vermont, as well as northward up the Connecticut Valley to White River Junction, Hanover, and beyond. Many of the popular fall foliage bus tours cross northern Vermont and swing down through the White Mountains.

Mountain Foliage

IF YOU ENJOY seeing and photographing entire mountain slopes ablaze with color, you can find much of it on Route 2 in Massachusetts, between Greenfield on the Connecticut River and Williamstown near the New York border. The route winds up and through the highest portion of the Berkshires, and there is much fine autumn hillside scenery in the vicinity of Shelburne Falls, Florida, and other communities. A two-mile drive on the turn-off road to Zoar, along the shore of the upper Deerfield River, can be photogenically rewarding. The Zoar Road is not numbered, but the turn-off sign "To Zoar" should catch your eye about four miles west of Charlemont.

The White Mountains display some of the finest autumn color in New England.

Route 2 reaches its highest point just above North Adams, where large-scale golden panoramas are possible. Columbus Day, or a day or two before, has always been just about the right time for photographing fall foliage in this area.

Don't make the mistake of thinking that the White Mountains are too high or too evergreen-covered for good autumn foliage. These mountains display some of the finest autumn color in New England. They are surprisingly concentrated with deciduous trees, with maples and birches growing far up on the high slopes. The valleys are deep and the southern slopes well sheltered from cold-front winds, so that fall color is only slightly earlier than in the areas southward. The cream of White Mountains foliage is perhaps along Route 302 as it curves down through Crawford Notch. If you hit it right, you'll find entire mountainsides glowing in rich gold, and often, some gems of autumn foliage along the banks of the infant Saco River, where groves of birch and maple bend over the rippling waters. The first week of October is usually the best time for this area, with some brilliant early color often showing up at September's end if the weather has been cool.

In Vermont, you'll find some superb color on the mountain slopes in the Bridgewater and Sherbourne areas, just east of Rutland. Route 4 eastward out of Rutland traverses a low pass in the Green Mountains and follows beautifully rolling country as it heads for the Connecticut River Valley, with many golden mountain slopes and color-bordered streams along the way. At West Bridgewater, a brief detour northward on Route 100 should prove well worth your while, as there are some extremely photogenic forest slopes near Sherbourne. For this region, we recommend a target date of about October 8, although you usually have plenty of leeway if stormy weather doesn't destroy early color.

In Vermont, you'll find some superb color on the mountain slopes in the Bridgewater and Sherbourne areas.

Route 11 and lower Route 7 will also traverse some fine mountain foliage, as will Route 9 between Bennington and Brattleboro. In northern Vermont, as in extreme northern New Hampshire and the Rangeley Lakes region of Maine, the mountain slopes are a bit more evergreen, and the leaves may turn as early as the last week in September, but do present autumnal beauty at their peak.

Autumn Foliage at Village, Lake, Stream, and Farm

ALTHOUGH THE golden mountain slopes are magnificent to behold, the most successful autumn photographs are often those of rural village scenes, old farms, winding country roads, and trees bordering millponds.

One of the most photogenic autumn back routes you can find is Route 123 westward from Marlow, New Hampshire, which is just north of Keene. This road winds through some storybook hamlets nestled in dips and dells of the woodlands, some with rushing mill streams, old bridges, and interesting twists and turns of road. In this region, clumps and single specimens of bright orange or red maples often stand in striking positions beside old barns or rushing streams. As we mention in the New Hampshire section, Marlow itself is a much-photographed gem. Here, a few plain white attractive village structures, including an old meeting house, are loosely gathered around a double millpond. Brilliant swamp maples and sugar maples cast their reflections along with the

houses; shooting through and between these trees, you can get some excellent photographs.

Much of southwestern New Hampshire is like this, and you'll find many colorful autumn scenes along Routes 9 and 10 and other routes out of Keene. Some of the covered bridges of this area, mentioned earlier, might provide excellent focal points for autumn photographs. This is not high altitude terrain, and peak foliage may come as late as October 15. You'll find that as you travel through much of New Hampshire and Vermont, foliage color will vary from county to county because of altitude. After driving through magnificent color for 20 minutes, you may dip into a valley and return to summer green. But this all helps to make the autumn foliage season longer. You may

A QUADRUPLE-TRUNKED ELM TREE, CASTINE, MAINE.

get the high-road shots, and those who come along the route a week or so later will get the valley shots.

In Vermont, Route 30 northwest out of Brattleboro through Newfane, or Route 4 west from White River Junction through Woodstock, will lead you to many photographic village and farm scenes.

Farther north, between Montpelier and the Connecticut River on Route 302, there are several side roads that present excellent foliage settings. We suggest Route 110 southward through Washington to Chelsea, returning to 302 by way of Corinth Corners, South Corners, and Route 25. The latter will take you through much-photographed Waits River and West Topsham, at their best in autumn.

In the lower Berkshires, in Massachusetts, there's always much good autumn foliage in the Lenox-Stockbridge region, especially along the many side roads that twist through this attractive countryside. At Lenox, the conspicuous white Church-on-the-Hill stands on its high point of land above a curve on Route 7, partly surrounded by maples that blaze brilliantly.

In the lower Berkshires, there's always much good autumn foliage in the Lenox-Stockbridge region.

Don't forget Connecticut — it's loaded with beautiful fall color spots. If you follow Route 7 down from the Berkshires, or northward from Danbury, you'll pass through some fine rustic stretches, particularly between Gaylordsville and Canaan. Here, where the road follows the Housatonic River, are some excellent views of photogenic foliage bordering water. The red covered bridge at West Cornwall blends nicely with the autumn color surrounding it. The bridge will catch your eye where Route 128 reaches Route 7, about 15 miles south of the Massachusetts border.

Litchfield's attractive village green is also at its best in the fall, and don't miss Candlewood and Squam Lakes, southward toward Danbury, when their shores are brilliant in unbroken orange. Color often peaks here as late as the third week of October. This is a good final point on your foliage tour, if you've been exploring Vermont and New Hampshire during the early part of the month.

In northeastern Connecticut, there are some surprise gems of autumn countryside. In the 20-mile stretch between Putnam, Connecticut, and Sturbridge, Massachusetts, along Routes 131 and 169, lies the Woodstock area, abounding in quiet country lanes, and attractive old villages, such as Quinebaug, on Route 131, and Woodstock, as well South and North Woodstock, on Route 169, all in Connecticut. There are many spots here where you'll find brilliant trees grouped beside stone walls, old ivied structures, or quiet brooklets.

Although Maine is not specifically noted for top autumn foliage when compared with Vermont or New Hampshire, it does present much autumnal beauty. Some of the best is in the western portion of the state; in particular, you'll find Route 26, as it heads northwest from Route 2 at Newry, rewarding. The road ascends gradually through granite mountains, sloped with both evergreen and autumn color in early October, and crosses several streams that are usually foliage-bordered. Just before it crosses Grafton Notch and dips sharply down into New Hampshire, the road passes Screw Auger Falls, which at peak foliage time presents some striking mixtures of rock, water, and color.

If you enter Maine from the Conways on Route 25 and come down through Lake Kezar and Kezar Falls, you'll find some excellent stretches of color, and the Bridgton-Pleasant Mountain area is extremely attractive in autumn. Many of the smaller ponds in this area, such as Moose Pond, on Route 302 between North Conway and Bridgton, present showy little settings where brilliant red or yellow trees bend over the water. Find your way to Route 133 and Wayne, and you'll discover a little village whose Main Street homes face a lake on each side, with plenty of golden foliage.

Wherever there are farms you'll find bright maples.

Although evergreens outnumber the deciduous trees as you go eastward and northward in Maine, the maples, birches, and other leafy types never entirely disappear. Wherever there are farms you'll find bright maples, and wherever there are lakes you'll always find at least one clump of red foliage leaning out over the water — particularly effective photographically if the leaves are touched by sun just breaking through the thick mist that rises off Maine lakes on many a brisk October morning.

Coastal and Southern New England Foliage

IF YOU SHOULD be intrigued by the rare sight of autumn foliage at the seashore, virtually bending over salt waves, there's a picnic turn-off on Route 1 just north of Rockland where many leafy maples and oaks line Clam Cove beach; here, you can photograph this rarity. Coastal autumn color is not bad at all in Maine, and if you follow Route 52 inland from Camden, it will skirt Megunticook Lake and pass a number of spots where calendar foliage photographs have been taken. A tip on photographing lakeshore color: get to a point near the most colorful tree, if you can, and shoot the general view with this tree dominating at the edge of the foreground.

Some final words about Maine foliage. Don't hesitate to view coastal foliage from the water if you have the opportunity. One of the short excursion boat trips available at the landing in Camden Harbor might well do it for you. The shore hills, particularly the Camden Hills viewed from Penobscot Bay, can present a beautiful picture from offshore. We heard one veteran lobsterman, long accustomed to the scene, comment on the beauty of the hills as viewed from his boat in October. The hills also look fine from the hills themselves. Drive to the top of Mount Battie for an excellent view of the surrounding lakes, hills, and wooded coastal headlands. Entrance to the drive is in Camden Hills State Park, on Route 1, immediately north of Camden.

Don't hesitate to view coastal foliage from the water if you have the opportunity.

In the coastal areas of southern New England — Cape Cod, Rhode Island, and the Long Island Sound shore of Connecticut — are many stretches of oak that do not present lively autumn color. These areas also tend to be flat, eliminating the enhancement of foliage that hills provide. Villages and farms near the coast do have color, however, and there's one big asset: the trees hold their color surprisingly late, affording the tardy traveler the chance to see foliage displays well after the inland trees are bare. In some areas, particularly in the Plymouth area and on Cape Cod, there are berry bushes and other small shrubs that will turn a brilliant red to beautify the landscape. Cranberry harvesting time, late September through October, is particularly colorful; the most concentrated displays are likely along Route 58, south of Plymouth off Route 44. Smaller, but equally brilliant, cranberry bogs may be seen at intervals as you drive eastward along Route 6A on Cape Cod between Sandwich and Dennis.

Inland in Rhode Island, particularly in the northwest corner, are rural areas with as much abundance of color as farm regions 300 miles farther north. On Route 94, you'll find brilliant sugar maples, singly and in clumps, tall birches, and rocky slopes covered with the red fire of underbrush. Two state parks near the Connecticut line in this region have ponds with nicely foliaged shores.

Autumn Weather in New England

THE WEATHER, which has a lot to do with the formation of top quality autumn foliage, is often a concern of those who come to photograph it. Much has been said of New England's changeable weather pattern, but on the *average*, October weather in New England is as nice as you'll find anywhere else in the eastern United States.

The autumn weather New Englanders hope for, and usually get for at least a week or two, is the delightful Indian summer variety. It is typified by hazy, placid, mild days, with cool misty mornings and touches of summer at midday. In its best form, it can continue for two weeks without interruption, right through the turning of autumn foliage, providing steady sunshine and, in general, making both travel and picture-taking highly enjoyable, although perhaps bestowing a diffusing haze over the landscape.

But jokes about New England weather are as old as its first settlements. In the fall, it is admittedly possible to encounter chains of showers or a spell of chill, blustery days, often beautifully clear for photog-

A ROADSIDE PUMPKIN SALE,
DEERFIELD, MASSACHUSETTS.

raphy but requiring warm clothing. Nature deals a hand and you play it as you can.

The average afternoon temperatures to be realistically expected on clear days during peak autumn foliage time range from the 50s in the White Mountains to the 70s in downtown Hartford. Subtract about 10° for cloudy days. Morning temperatures may dip briefly into the 30s but will usually rise rapidly as the sun moves above the hills. Extremes might surprise you. Long spells of Indian summer will occasionally push afternoon temperatures in the Connecticut valley to 80°, and Bangor, Maine, seldom regarded as a bit of the tropics, officially recorded 86° at midafternoon on October 16, 1968. But don't expect weather of this kind outside of the record books — especially, don't expect Bangor to ever, ever do that again! There have been a number of times when autumn foliage travelers have found snow covering the golden sugar maple leaves. Our advice can only be to come prepared for the average, but be poised for possible surprises.

WINTER

To many photographers, winter in New England is the prime time of the year — offering ski slopes, frozen waterfalls, village lanes enhanced by glistening white snow, ice carnivals, ice boat racing, and so on. If you don't mind standing or walking around in the cold, there's clearly a wealth of photography at hand in a New England winter.

First, a word about the winter itself. It's not always quite as bad as you may have been led to believe, and in this modern, heavily mechanized age, few places are ever snow-bound for any length of time, and few roads are ever unplowed for long. I seem to surprise people when I mention that I commuted 12 miles to work on the Maine coast for nine years without ever missing a day because of weather. Where there are fewer streets and fewer cars, controlling winter is less of a problem.

Perhaps the chief thing to remember about winter weather in New England is that however severe a

WINTER ON HIGH STREET, WARREN, MAINE.

cold snap may be, it's usually much milder along the coast than inland. We've seen differences of 30° within 20 miles, moving inland from the coast in Maine. Although the contrasts farther south are less dramatic, Boston is a lot milder than the Berkshires, 120 miles to the west of it, and Cape Cod, sticking right out into the ocean, can be in the 40s while the rest of the Northeast is sunk in deep freeze.

Inland, northern New England does get cold, and 25° below zero at least once a winter is not unusual. Moreover, when cold fronts race in from Canada, temperatures in northern New England will plummet with a rapidity rarely observed in city areas to the south. But New England weather varies greatly from week to week and year to year. There are mild winters when rain and mud prevail more often than snow and ice; there are January thaws so strong people worry about plants making false starts; and there are winters when ski areas without artificial snow-making equipment have worrisome years. Be prepared for snow and cold, but don't necessarily count on it.

Be prepared for snow and cold, but don't necessarily count on it.

Winter travel in New England need not be considered troublesome. Main roads are plowed so promptly when it snows that there is little chance of being stranded. Any motel you visit along the highways will keep its parking areas clear of snow. The chief hazards or nuisances in pursuing winter photography in New England are possible ice patches on side roads or the endless lines of plowed snow along the roads that prevent you from pausing where you'd like to.

Walking, sometimes very strenuously in deep snow, is very much a part of winter photography. You walk to get away from plowed places and plow piles; you walk to reach a vantage point; and you walk long distances from your car because the snow prevents you from parking at a handy location. Do wear boots of some kind, even if you don't intend to walk in snow, because you'll very likely wind up doing so anyway. And do have warm gloves. Use a cable release on your camera and you might be able to take pictures without removing the gloves — a very important asset when it's really cold. And always keep a shovel in your car. No matter how careful you are, you'll eventually park in some lane or other where in trying to turn around, you'll slide into a snow bank. But also be prepared to thoroughly enjoy the exhilarating feeling of walking in tangy air with glistening snow around you.

If you want to be reasonably sure of encountering a blanket of snow, and one not likely to soften until spring, visit lower Vermont and the White Mountains region of New Hampshire. Winter precipitation is fairly heavy there, and the land is seldom free of snow between Christmas and April. Snow comes earlier in western New England and tends to melt earlier; seacoast regions tend to have later winters because of lingering ocean warmth in late fall.

Nothing enhances tall church towers and the traditional New England village scene more than a complete blanket of snow. The campus at Williams College in Williamstown, Massachusetts, or at Dartmouth College in Hanover, New Hampshire, are at their photogenic peak in snow — Dartmouth, particularly, during their famous ice carnival.

The much-photographed villages of Waits River on Route 25 and Peacham in between Routes 302 and 2 in northern Vermont, or Whitefield in New Hampshire, on Route 3, 12 miles north of Franconia Notch, become Christmas card scenes under snow. If you don't mind hiking up a snowy hill in zero-degree weather (and the sky is usually the clearest blue, the snow surface the smoothest white in such weather), you can get some excellent shots of villages of this kind. And remember, if you hike up a hill in deep snow, whether at a ski slope or in an open area, move laterally far enough so that your bootprints don't show in the photograph.

Covered bridges are particularly enhanced by snow. Few winter scenes are more eye-catching than a red covered bridge with snow atop and snow-laden branches bending over the shore of a dark, turbulent, partly frozen stream, perhaps with protruding rocks that are white with snow. I'm thinking now of that West Cornwall bridge over the Housatonic River in Connecticut, where there are both a woodsy shore and red coloring. By the way, if you should head that way just to visit the bridge, it's in West Cornwall, where Route 128 meets Route 7, not in Cornwall Bridge. People are sometimes confused by the town names, but the town of Cronwall Bridge, four miles south of West Cornwall, has nothing more photogenic than a modern steel highway bridge.

A word here about winter shots over water. Early winter, just after the first snow has fallen, is usually the best time for these. Lakes and streams are still unfrozen, and the scenic contrast between snow and water is doubly attractive. Later in the season, water surfaces may freeze and become as white as the shore, erasing your contrast and making the pond or river look like a snowy meadow.

The ponds in and around cities may remain snow-

Few winter scenes are more eye-catching than a red covered bridge with snow atop.

free much of the winter. The big lakes of the north, however, such as the Rangeley Lakes in Maine, freeze early and freeze deep. At Mooselookmeguntic Lake, we have seen the cracking and buckling of enormously deep ice in mid-April — breaking ice so thick that it looked like concrete blocks. In that region, ice-out guessing contests are sometimes not decided until well into May.

THE CAMDEN SNOW BOWL, CAMDEN, MAINE.

Winter Sports

WINTER SPORTS are photogenic gems, if you don't mind spending a lot of time out in the cold. Action skiing shots are always exciting and a challenge, but you've got to be dressed at least as warmly as the skiers — remember, they are consistently active while you're often standing still — and you'll need those previously mentioned boots. If you're any kind of skier yourself, by all means come down the slope as carefully as you can with your camera and pause at any point along the trail or slope that offers good photographic potential. Remember that the slope in your picture must be steep enough to be obvious and that the skier should be turning or crossing a mogul — sending up snow spray if possible — so as to appear to be in rapid motion. All too often, photos of moving skiers look like posed stills.

You can enhance your ski slope photos by including some of the scenic background that is almost always available at ski areas: forest, rising mountains, or a farther bend of the ski trail itself. If you want to photograph a general impression of a ski area, rather than a skier in action, you can often get some excellent shots from the ski lifts or the cafeteria decks, looking down on people readying to ski, groups of skiers at racks, or skiers boarding gondolas.

Most ski slopes are in mountainous regions and provide great views from their heights. Camden Snow Bowl, on the Maine coast in Camden, has views out to sea and across lakes to steep mountain edges. At several ski slopes in the White Mountains, the upper slopes provide grand vistas particularly at Cannon Mountain, where I-93 reaches Franconia Notch, and Wildcat Mountain, on Route 16, very close to Glen Ellis Falls and the Mount Washington Auto Road. The lower areas provide fine mountain shots whichever way you face.

Other winter sports, such as skating on ponds, make excellent shots, although ponds are sometimes surprisingly hard to find, because many ponds freeze unevenly or become snow-covered early on. Ice boating can be interesting too, but it's not the most widely practiced of winter sports. Lake Bomoseen in Vermont, on U.S. 4 between Rutland and the New York State line, has from time to time been a center for iceboat racing. And at Rangeley, Maine, where there are 100 miles of snowmobile trails, there's also an annual dog sled race in March that can easily arouse a photographer's enthusiasm.

Light and Cold Effects

WINTER PHOTOGRAPHY does differ in a few ways from photography in other seasons, chiefly where lighting is concerned. On the one hand, the sunlight is weaker and, on the other hand, sunlit surfaces are made abnormally brilliant by snow cover. A snowy expanse can play havoc with traditional exposures. Be sure to use your meter — and use it cautiously.

Your camera's built-in meter will tend to react strongly to background brilliance, thereby misreading a foreground object on which you may be focusing. Shots of skiers are often faulted by silhouetting.

The low angle of the sun in winter can increase problems, particularly at ski slopes. Most ski slopes descend northward, and at noon in December or January you may find that you can't point your camera upslope without aiming it directly into the sun. To photograph descending skiers, find a spot on a bending trail or slope where you can aim eastward or westward. Get sun on the skiers' faces if at all possible. Morning is perhaps the best time for ski photography.

If you're just photographing winter landscapes, don't hesitate to await approaching sunset. As in other seasons, the close-to-setting sun will add a suggestion of gold to your scene that is particularly effective on white drifts or snow-covered fields. When photographing close to buildings at this time of year, the shadow areas are often so broad and so dark in comparison to sunny or snowy patches that you'll need to plan photos with care. Generally, unless you can take a subject entirely in sun or entirely in shade, don't make the attempt. Yes, flash is a solution. As most professional photographers have always done in contrasting light situations, use a flash to illuminate the shady side of a face or an object. It can do wonders, just as it can help in close-ups of flowers at warmer times of the year.

Winter brings opportunities for many special effects and unusual shots. In some areas, fountains or springs freeze into towers of natural ice sculpture. At some ski areas, such as Mohawk Mountain in Connecticut, on Route 4, five miles east of Cornwall Bridge, where natural springs supply the fountains, astonishingly tall ice towers have resulted. And we've all seen the run-off streams in the mountains that coat highway passes with ice, particularly where blasting has produced sheer cliffs. The largest such mass of ice we've seen was on Route 2 above North Adams in Massachusetts, where rocky ledges were covered with what resembled a frozen Niagara.

When temperatures dip to zero or below, thick fog wisps rise from unfrozen water. The most dramatic of these we've ever seen were on the Maine coast during the record-breaking cold of early 1971, when eerie fog spirals rose like thick smoke from the surface of Penobscot Bay. If you are near the sea when sub-zero cold strikes, you might like to try to photograph this "sea smoke," as it is called. It's not an easy

Morning is perhaps the best time for ski photography.

MORNING MIST OVER A BROOK
IN BANTAM, CONNECTICUT.

job — you'll freeze your fingers stiff, for one thing, if you don't work fast, and the exposure has to be just right or the mist will look like smudges on your print (or hardly be visible at all). When taking pictures in bitter cold, keep in mind that your shutter may be slower than the speed for which it is set.

Snowy or icy trees are perhaps the most purely beautiful subjects in winter photography. For great success you do need luck here, in the sense that nature must participate in the timing. Snow-lined branches should dazzle in bright sunlight, preferably with deep blue sky behind them, but it doesn't always happen that way. So often, those instances when snow clings to every twig occur at evening or under continuing cloudiness, and before you get sunlight, wind or rising temperature can demolish your subjects at a fast rate.

Whenever you do find bright sunlight on snowy trees, get your camera to work immediately. Again be careful of your exposure; remember that the prime element you are photographing is sunlit white snow. Try to find one or two specific trees to focus on; unless you're fairly distant from them, a group of trees may appear a bit jumbled in a photograph. And again, approach your subject by a careful route; don't

spoil the pristine smoothness of a fresh cover of snow by getting your own bootprints in the picture.

Finally, where winter photography is concerned, don't forget children sledding down a hill — a scene you might of course be able to find near your home as well as in northern New England or a park in Hartford or Boston. All you need is a snowfall and a bunch of kids. This is the kind of shot local editors might by happy to use.

MAIN STREET, WARREN, MAINE.

LOBSTER HARBOR NEAR
OWLS HEAD, MAINE.

SPRING

Spring most anywhere is an upbeat season, especially to those who love to travel or partake of outdoor activity. Many people who can manage to do so "hit the road" at the first breath of a warm breeze or the first bright buds of green. Photographers, eager to get going again, unfailingly notice that the sunlight is brighter, the shadow areas shorter, and the days longer. The sun is, after all, as high in the sky in the third week in April as it is in the third week of August, albeit shining down on a land just out of the grip of winter, rather than one already in the warm grip of summer.

But despite the bright sunshine and inviting green, some people may ask what there is to see, do, or photograph in New England in spring. The beaches are still too cold for use, most of the tourist attractions remain closed, and even a good number of the

PEAR BLOSSOMS.

state parks are not yet open. Moreover, isn't much of northern New England plagued in spring by plain, old-fashioned mud?

In truth, there is much to see and do — and photograph — in virtually all of New England in spring. The mud? It is short-lived and of nuisance chiefly to farmers and rural homeowners who find their driveways and yard areas a bit soft, but not to the traveler on paved highways or town streets. The only discouraging thing mud does to people with cameras is deprive them at times of the joy of photographing a key waterfall.

No doubt about it, waterfalls are at their photogenic best in spring, when they sometimes carry twice the water they do in late summer. By all means visit those that you can; the ones that you can drive up close to with parking on gravel and approach on firm paths. Trails that require hiking into the woods and up mountain slopes, such as those to Arethusa and Ripley Falls in New Hampshire, may well be closed. Hikers on spring hillside paths often find themselves losing traction on a muddy surface, slipping on wet stones, and at times crossing a wide shallow brook where there's not usually any brook. If you're eager to get to one of those burgeoning forest or mountain falls in spring, check with local state park personnel and perhaps you'll receive encouraging news that will enable you to go ahead.

There is much to see and do in virtually all of New England in spring.

In southern New England, the business of warming after winter gets underway more promptly than in the northern reaches. The ocean edge will be a bit slow in warming, but Connecticut, Rhode Island, and much of Massachusetts are rid of mud and ice early, and the flowers promptly bloom with gusto. A number of parks, public gardens, and arboretums here can give as colorful a display as many of those in the southern states. The early May garden tour in Boston's Beacon Hill neighborhood might surprise you with the display of magnolias.

Spring Parks and Gardens

SPRING IS AN ideal time to visit Boston for almost any reason. It may not quite be Paris, but Boston in the spring has spirit-freshening bursts of green and bloom along the Charles River and in Boston Common and the Public Garden that can enhance any outdoor photograph. In the suburbs south of the city, the Arnold Arboretum at Jamaica Plain provides excellent displays of flowering plants and shrubs.

In other cities, there are parks that offer flower and nature subject matter. In Connecticut, the Bartlett Arboretum, on Route 137 just north of Stamford, is a gem, as is the huge Connecticut College Arboretum, in New London. If you happen to be in Hartford, Elizabeth and Bushnell Parks are worth looking into for their bursting of spring. In Rhode Island, Blithewold Gardens and Arboretum, in Bristol, has much in the way of photogenic gardening aspects, with a little of everything from picturesque rock gardens to bamboo groves. The wealth of delightful and imaginative specimens of plant sculpture to be found in the topiary at Green Animals Garden in Portsmouth, Rhode Island, might intrigue you into taking a fair amount of pictures, especially if you have children with you.

In the Bershires, spring is ushered in with proud displays at the Bershire Garden Center, on Route 102 just outside Stockbridge. Here there's plenty to attract your camera — ponds with lilies, many varieties of flowering plants, an excellent herb garden, and a greenhouse with tropical exotics. Nearby Naumkeag Gardens also has much to photograph, although it is more formally landscaped.

Patriot's Day is the best time of year to visit Concord and Lexington.

Patriot's Day in Massachusetts

PATRIOT'S DAY IS A prime spring holiday in Massachusetts. Honoring the anniversary of the start of the American Revolution, it is usually celebrated the third Monday in April. There is much historical pageantry to be viewed at various places on this day, but if you're in Boston, crowds and attention will also be focused on the annual Boston Marathon.

Patriot's Day is the best time of year to visit Concord and Lexington, where parades and pageantry are always conducted on this day, including a stirring reenactment of the battle scene at Lexington Battle Green on Interstate 95, take Exit 30 to Route 2A and go east to Lexington or west to Concord. If you're ever wanted to travel back in time with your camera and capture historical events on film, this is your chance. With soldiers in red uniform, colonial farmers in period clothing, the smoke of battle in the air, and a number of those sturdy white residences standing in the background just as they did in 1775, who will notice a few power lines or a couple of Stop and No Right Turn signs?

At nearby Concord, there are further bits of historical reenactment and, of course, the famous Minuteman Statue at North Bridge, which has perhaps been photographed almost as often over the years as the Washington Monument and the Statue of Liberty. Nearby Walden Pond offers not only a tranquil view of the spring greening of a New England lake shore, but also a look at the site of Henry David Thoreau's cabin. Both Concord and Lexington display a number of large old stately homes that not only date back to Revolutionary days, but were lived in by prominent literary and political figures of their day.

On Long Island Sound and in Narragansett Bay, cruise fishing schedules begin by early May. Particularly check Niantic and Waterford, on Route 156 west of New London, Connecticut, Groton and Mystic, on Route 1 east of New London, and Narragansett, on Route 1A just east of Wakefield, Rhode Island. All offer good wharf shots even if you don't fish.

Spring in Northern New England

IN EARLIER SPRING, there are some photographic opportunities in the cooler northern areas that can't be encountered in many spots elsewhere. If massive ice interests you, for example, some interesting photographs may be had of ice breaking on the big northern lakes such as the Rangeley Lakes and Moosehead Lake in Maine, or Lake Memphremagog, in Vermont, on I-91 at Newport, close to the Canadian border. At the Rangeley Lakes, ice-break usually occurs in mid- to late April. One year, on April 15th, the ice breaking up at the head of Mooselookmeguntic Lake at Haines Landing, at the very end of Route 4, west of Oquossoc village, was a fantastic jumble of giant slabs two or three feet thick. They were tilted at odd angles, sometimes grinding and slipping with pools and trickles of icewater showing here and there between them. Contests at Rangeley and at other lakes offer prizes for those who guess the ice-out date correctly. For the Rangeley Lakes, the winning date has often been after the first of May, even though temperatures by that time have reached the 70s in meadows away from the water. Sights like this make you realize how easily an ice age might come upon us if the sun did not maintain its schedule.

Maple sugaring is a very early spring task. There are many maple sugar groves throughout New England, chiefly in Vermont, perhaps, but also a goodly number elsewhere (even though much of the

In earlier spring, there are some photographic opportunities in the cooler northern areas that can't be encountered in many spots elsewhere.

maple syrup is merchanded through Vermont simply because consumers throughout the country prefer syrup with a Vermont label). March is really the month for maple syrup in Vermont, and if you want a place where you can watch or photograph the process, we suggest the area around Stowe, Vermont, at Route 100, north of Waterbury, or eastward from there to St. Johnsbury, where Interstate 91, Interstate 93, and U.S. 2 meet. Although much of the tapping and processing is accomplished on what amounts to various people's farms, there are locations each year where viewing is possible, although locations may differ from year to year. Check tourist information centers in Stowe, Montpelier, and Burlington for updated details.

Ever since Currier and Ives, maple sugar time has been popular pictorially, and never a spring goes by without a few new magazine articles depicting the various stages of sugaring, including colorful shots of well-bundled people tapping tree trunks in the snow, or hauling sap to barns and sheds on horse-drawn sleds. The big Maple Grove sugar plant in St. Johnsbury, the largest of its kind in the United States, offers tours of the sugar processing rooms. The

AN ANNUAL SPRING EVENT: NETTING ALEWIVES IN WARREN, MAINE

adjoining museum provides a wealth of information, tools, and photographs pertaining to the whole deal of getting sap out of sugar maples and turning it into such popular. products as breakfast syrup.

Later in the spring, if you'd like to catch a spring sunrise without being too alone on a mountain top, there are a number of sunrise services on Easter Sunday. A notable one takes place annually atop Mount Snow in southern Vermont. And if it's possible to take pictures in or of fast-moving canoes, an event such as East Burke's white water canoe race in early May in Vermont would provide you the opportunity.

All in all, spring is not a bad time to be visiting New England. The cities and the gardens are certainly at their best, as are many of the historical sites. And if you want to visit key tourist centers and have them pretty much to yourself, spring is the time. You can get shots that might be marred or delayed at other times by encroaching traffic or parked vehicles.

One thing about spring often delights and permeates your daily mood, particularly if you're a roaming outdoor type: a strong awareness that this is the "beginning." You are at scenic spots ahead of everyone else, and if you are enjoying yourself, you're just beginning a year of such enjoyment and activity. You've brushed aside the cobwebs of winter, broken out of your shell, and are breathing deeply of the fresh air of a new season.

MAINE

The Coast

Think Maine coast and at least three of the key scenic or much-photographed elements of New England come to mind: lighthouses standing atop lonely cliffs; weatherbeaten wharves bedecked with lobster traps reaching out into rocky harbors, and long combers of surf breaking majestically on granite shores. There are also picturesque coves studded with sailing craft, and neat, wind-swept villages where venerable clapboard houses stand austerely in the sun. All of these things are still at hand, if you don't let the coast's complicated geography hide them from view or lure you to the end of the wrong peninsula.

First, a general word on what the Maine coast is or is not, and what kind of territory you're entering if you've never been there before. The Maine coast is not southern California in style, nor is it a somnolent museum piece dozing in the mists. It is a highly

A LOBSTERMAN'S WHARF, ASH POINT.

diversified stretch of modern America — the very new mixed with the very old, the vacation life overlapping with the nine-to-five life, and no two towns alike in appearance or personality.

If some of the coastal towns surprise you with their size and the extent of their older business and residential districts, it should be remembered that the coast of Maine through the years has not been just a rustic string of lobstering ports and salt farms. A century or more ago it was a major lumbering and boat-building center; Bath, Thomaston, Belfast, and other towns were large and prospering before the Civil War, and the Penobscot River was once one of the busiest commercial waterways in the United States.

Today in the older communities of the Maine coast, this era is well remembered. Many homes are handsomely furnished with proudly preserved pieces of nineteenth-century furniture, handed down through the generations from the days of the sea captains and the men who built the great four-masters. Local historical societies eagerly keep the past alive, cataloging the old photographs, brushing the old cemetery stones, marking the sites of earliest landings and settlers. The past, one might say, is not buried in textbooks, it's visible right down the street.

Lighthouses

THOSE WHO CHERISH the past often bemoan the fact that many of the old lighthouses are now out of service, replaced by unglamorous steel shafts. But whether still in service or not, the more colorful towers still stand. Some of the smaller ones are privately owned now, but some of the larger ones are more accessible to the public than they were in their active years.

If you have hoped to see and photograph a "typical" Maine lighthouse, we're happy to say there are a number that roughly fit the description.

If you have hoped to see and photograph a "typical" Maine lighthouse, standing on a clifftop with dark, sharp-pointed trees behind it and white surf far below, we're happy to say there are a number that roughly fit the description. In fact, there are some notable ones that you can drive or walk right up to and photograph from various angles.

Pemaquid Point lighthouse is the most frequently visited of these. It stands at the tip end of the Pemaquid peninsula (eastward on Route 130 from Damariscotta or on Route 32 from Waldoboro), surrounded by park land, with ample parking space. In front of the lighthouse, broken ledges of limestone and granite shelve down to the Atlantic breakers.

One spiny ridge fingers well outward, ending at a
high dome young people love to climb, be it precari-
ous or not. On any of the lower rocky shelves you
can photograph breaking waves, odd rock formations, constantly encircling gulls, and, of course, the
lighthouse, rising above it all.

At the grass atop the rocky slope you can walk
completely around the lighthouse and photograph it
against either the sky or the sea, or along the edge of
the white picket fence that borders it on one side.
Swooping gulls are ever present, and once in a while

PEMAQUID POINT
LIGHTHOUSE.

one will perch for you on the very tip of the tower. The best time to photography the lighthouse is perhaps before sunset, when the lowering rays will add a touch of golden cream to the pale sides of the tower and the shadow lines are stronger. To get lighthouse, rocks, and sea all in one shot, climb laboriously eastward over the rocks to a point just below the restaurant that stands east of the parking field. We suggest doing this in morning or at mid-day, as you'll be pointing your camera westward.

Owls Head lighthouse is on Penobscot Bay and seldom has dramatic surf at its base, but its position on a steep headland is the archetypical lighthouse scene. It too stands in a park, but this park is much less frequented and publicized than the one at Pemaquid. If you don't mind a long stroll from your parked car, this is a peaceful, scenic spot in which to relax with your camera. Drive south on Route 73 from Route 1 in downtown Rockland, and Owls Head is the next community. When you reach the town's little lobster harbor, turn left around the harbor's rim, and you'll come to the parking field for the lighthouse park. A path winds through groves of trees to the lighthouse and the downward glimpses of rocky coves and pebbly beaches to your right along the way are themselves highly photogenic. "Keep Back; Sheer Cliff" say the signs along the path, and people invariably run over to see what sort of cliff they're supposed to stay back from. There's one spot on this cliff where you can get as fine a shot of a lighthouse with the sea below as you might find on any respectable calendar. It has, in fact, appeared on many calendars and coastal tourist brochures. At the lighthouse itself, a panoramic view over the water opens before you and there is a grassy, spruce-shaded knoll from which to shoot.

West Quoddy Head lighthouse is the easternmost structure in the United States and stands candy-striped in a tidy green lawn atop a 50-foot cliff — a lighthouse in the grand tradition, with a rugged landscape around it. Its location is called "west" despite its position, simply because it's on the west side of an inlet to Passamaquoddy Bay, which has its east side on Campobello Island in Canada. Here too there is a park — a comparatively large state park, with paths that wind to the high cliffs west of the light, affording a broad range of rocky seascapes. Below the lighthouse there is a beach with a seemingly endless expanse of smoothly rounded stones of all sizes and colors. Tall turrets of dark rock rise somewhat mysteriously to enhance the surf that swirls between them.

To reach the lighthouse and accompanying West Quoddy Head State Park, turn off Route 189 into South Lubec Road on the outskirts of Lubec. (The turn is prominently marked "To West Quoddy Head."

The public is welcome to walk up to the lighthouse, where there's an attractive lawn, a white fence, and a striking view across the turbulent tidal waters to Campobello Island. Far out to sea, on clear days, the stark cliffs of another Canadian island, Grand Manan, may be seen as a pale gray wall along

THE LIGHTHOUSE AT WEST QUODDY HEAD NEAR LUBEC, MAINE, THE EASTERNMOST POINT OF LAND IN THE UNITED STATES.

the horizon. Quoddy Head is a cool place — you can shiver here when it's broiling hot a few miles inland, and you may find fog here while Route 1 is in sunshine — but in any mood it presents numerous photographic opportunities.

Nubble Light at Cape Neddick, a very short drive on Route 1 from York Beach, 10 miles north of Kittery, has long been a calendar favorite, standing amid white rocks as though carefully placed as an example in subject composition. Unfortunately, as its public access has recently been cut off by private lands, you can't walk up to this one. What you *can* do is walk to the foot of Nubble Road, at the north end of York Beach, and photograph across a narrow inlet.

Some lighthouses are on islands, and you need a boat to reach them. In Rockport harbor, for example, little Indian Island lighthouse, privately owned, makes a striking picture from the water. There is also **Cuckold Light,** on an island off the Boothbays, often photographable from excursion boats out of Boothbay Harbor, although you can also catch it with a telephoto lens from the end of Route 27 at

Newagen. But the king of island lighthouses is **Bass Harbor Light** at the southern end of Mount Desert Island, often pictured in books, magazines, and calendars, but virtually photographable only from the water — unless you do some mountain goat-like balancing on rocks along the shore. This lighthouse is much admired by yachtspeople and small-boat

sailors, as well as by calendar publishers. The Swan
Island ferry out of Bass Harbor sails past it. By land,
it's on its own little road, off Alternate Route 102 just
east of Bass Harbor.

At **Grindel Point**, where the ferry from Lincolnville Beach, on Route 1 north of Camden, docks at
Islesboro island in Penobscot Bay, there's a small
commercially owned lighthouse that is open to the
public for a moderate fee. Climb to the rail at its top,
and there's a nice view across the bay to the Camden
Hills.

Portland Head Light, at the entrance to Portland
Harbor, has been well photographed from the sea,
and although you can get to it by land, on Route 77
just east of South Portland, the grounds are open
only at specified days and hours.

PEMAQUID POINT.

Ocean Surf

MANY PEOPLE accustomed to surf on sandy beaches seek an on-the-rocks version when they come to Maine, but find the open Atlantic deceptively elusive east of Portland. So many roads to the shore seem to end at calm waters where offshore island serve as breakwaters. Some road maps are unintentionally deceptive in that they omit many of these islands and give the impression that towns in sheltered waters, such as Tenants Harbor or Port Clyde, are actually on the edge of the open ocean, which they are not. Motels on the shores of bays such as Penobscot often advertise "on the ocean," much to the disappointment of any visiting surf lover. The elusive breakers of the true Atlantic are best found at peninsula tips such as **Pemaquid**, **Cape Elizabeth**, or **Schoodic Point**.

Schoodic Point, on the mainland portion of Acadia National Park, just south of Gouldsboro, at the National Park entrance on Route 186, is much the same type of place as Pemaquid — a rugged, rocky shore where waves seldom break the same way twice. Here, shooting at a tangent across the breakers, it is possible to include the mountains of Mount Desert Island in your background. There's a miniature canyon at Schoodic into which waves surge with interesting effect, sending spray soaring high into the air. Closer to the larger towns, Two Lights Park, on Cape Elizabeth, just outside of Portland, presents strong surf on rocks, though the shore here is straighter, less complex, and broken.

Rocky oceanfronts such as those at Pemaquid and Schoodic present very massive stage sets for breakers. Domes and crags close to the water's edge are often deceptively huge, and therefore tend to make average breakers seem small in photographs. In the calm weather that often prevails in June or July, wave action may disappoint you. But if you visit these locations a day or two after the first fall northeaster, or after any severe coastal storm, the huge rollers that crash over those rocks and send spray towering should definitely quicken your eagerness to take pictures.

When photographing waves, by all means avoid strong wind from the salt spray toward your camera. Fortunately, on most of the clearer days the wind is from the west, more or less at your back. It's a good practice at any seashore to keep your camera under cover between shots, as protection against salt spray.

Wave pictures at any time require patience. Waves

will often stop breaking once you are set and ready, and the greatest breaker you ever saw will crash the moment you pause to reload. But be patient and you'll eventually get your shot. Don't just wait for the crash and spray; some of the more dramatic waves pictorially are those caught just *before* they break, showing the streaks and lines of power and motion.

Be careful for yourself as well as your camera when seas are high. When you're perched on a long finger of rock, you can't run away from that one wave in ten or so that's twice as big as the others and suddenly looms before you. The sea at Pemaquid, for one, *has* killed photographers. Above all, wear soft-soled shoes when walking out on those rocks; you will not be secure in hard-soled street shoes.

You don't need enormous waves, of course, to take beautiful seascapes. Take the drive along the outer rim of Acadia National Park, close between the mountains and the sea. Here there are numerous magnificent sea views, often from atop high cliffs, and there are curving, semihidden coves with pebbly beaches that you can look down into. This shoreline doesn't directly face the marching swells, and spectacular breakers may not be seen except after storms, but when the seas are at all high, the famous "Blowhole" — a natural attraction near the Bar Harbor end of the road, where waves enter a cave and come up like geysers through a break in the stone — should not be missed.

You don't need enormous waves to take beautiful seascapes.

Conventional breakers on sandy beaches may be seen, photographed, and bathed in at Kennebunk, Ogunquit, York, Wells, and Orchard Beaches, which are strung out along Route 1 between Kittery and Portland. There are some fine grassy dunes at Kennebunk Beach, where you may find an occasional sand rose in bloom. At Popham Beach, seaward on Route 209 from Route 1 at Bath, there is a mixed pattern of sandy beach and rocky shore with interesting sandspits and tidal effects.

Turn seaward from Route 1 at Milbridge in Washington County, and after a few miles you'll come to McClellan Park, an out-of-the-way surprise. This is one of those really scenic gems. Here you can stand on lonely rocky ledges and look far out to sea, with craggy islands of various sizes and shapes in the waters before you and interesting rock formations around you.

Lobstering

LOBSTERING CONTRIBUTES much to the photogenic mystique of Maine — the moored white lobster boats, the weather-beaten wharves, the stacks of lobster traps, and the rows of marker buoys flashing various colors in the sun.

To photograph traps, buoys, and wharves in one closely knit setting, visit New Harbor on Route 32 on the way to Pemaquid Point, no doubt the most photographed lobster cove in Maine. You've seen it on dozens of calendars, in magazine advertisements, and

perhaps even on television commercials. Here you can photograph much interesting harbor activity from a wharf-top seafood restaurant, sometimes including a lobsterman unloading his catch or taking on pails of fish bait.

BAY POINT.

Perhaps the most attractive of the real, nitty-gritty lobster ports — the kind with no restaurants or tourist shops — is Friendship, a few miles south of Waldoboro on Route 220, or south from Warren on 97. Here is a series of working lobster wharves finger out into a little harbor, and there's nothing going on but lobstering.

Many other villages and coves along the coast have

lobstering sights and sounds. To name a few: Owls Head and Spruce Head, on Route 73 south from Route 1 in Rockland; Port Clyde, at the end of Route 131 south from Route 1 at Thomaston (also reachable from Route 73, which joins Route 131); Stonington, at the end of Route 15 south from Route 1 at Orland; Vinalhaven, reached by ferry from the Route 1 terminal in Rockland; and South Bristol, on Route 129, which branches off from Route 130 just south of Route 1 at Damariscotta. All of these towns have additional features ranging from old houses and sunken vessels to a little drawbridge at South Bristol. There are boatbuilding shops in many of the lobstering communities, and you may catch interesting shots of planking being applied to a shapely hull, right out on the shore.

Sailing Craft

FRIENDSHIP, AS WELL as being a busy lobstering port, is also the home of the affectionately admired Friendship sloops — the sturdy, broad-beamed, but easily maneuvered craft used by lobstermen in pre-gasoline days. The Friendship Sloop Society, whose members have preserved or restored many of the old originals from pre-World War I days and have built a few new ones in replica, is headquartered here. Their colorful regatta, once held annually in Friendship, but in recent years in Boothbay Harbor — on Route 27 north from Route 1 at Wiscasset — about 14 miles west on Route 1 from Friendship's Route 220 — affords one of the best opportunities anywhere to photograph an abundance of sloops under sail. The races themselves, usually held on three successive days in the last week of July, are viewable only from boats, but on the final day of the regatta, all participating sloops parade under sail past wharves and reviewing stands. There are few sights prettier than 40 sloops coming right at you in single file and neatly turning one by one to pass at an easy stone's throw. Excursion craft carry spectators out to the racing scene, and excellent shots of boats turning sharply past markers in a brisk breeze can sometimes be gained from them, especially by telephoto lens.

Another sailing event of long standing is the annual Retired Skippers' race out of Castine, on Route 175, south from Route 1 at Orland. The race is held every August (dates vary), and the picturesque old village of Castine takes on a festive air for this event. Start and finish can be photographed by telephoto lens from Dice Head, the parklike clifftop west of the village center. There are many fine old houses, churches, and historical sites in Castine to hold your interest while awaiting termination of the boat race.

The Photogenic Old Towns

IF YOU'RE AN OLD house buff, or want to photograph houses that date to the early 1800s or late 1700s, there are ample opportunities on the Maine coast. The countryside and the villages are strewn with more older houses than realized at first glance, as houses lived in and maintained don't often show their age outwardly.

One of the largest collections of fine old houses to be found anywhere in New England is in Bath, on Route 1, 35 miles east of Portland. If you head north through the Bath business district you'll enter an area of handsome homes of the past that goes on for approximately a mile. In contrast, on the other side of town, Bath Iron Works, the big shipbuilding plant, displays one of the world's heftiest marine cranes —

DAMARISCOTTA MILLS.

a modern landmark that towers over the town and may be photographed best from the walkway of the Route 1 bridge across the Kennebec River (in early morning or late afternoon, if you want to avoid the silhouetting that kills its coloring much of the day).

Portland has many fine old homes as well, though they are separated a bit by newer city construction, and a fine assortment of handsome brick churches and historic mansions. The best way to get into Portland is to take I-295 (which veers off from I-95 as you approach the city from either north or south) and turn off into the downtown area at Exit 5 or 6. As in all busy cities, it is wise to avoid entering during rush hour. Some of the key buildings worth seeing and photographing are the Morse-Libby House at 109 Danforth Street; Tate House at 487 Westbrook Street; and the Wadsworth-Longfellow House at 487 Congress Street. Don't try to locate these addresses by pure exploration — it's a big town. The Office of Tourism at 142 Free Street will gladly come to your aid with maps and brochures galore.

Other towns that have their fair share of old houses include York, on Route 1, or via I-95, 10 miles north of the New Hampshire state line; South Berwick, on Route 4 at the New Hampshire state line, just east of Dover, New Hampshire; Kennebunk and Kennebunkport, on Route 1 or via I-95, 15 miles north of York; Belfast, on Route 1 north of Camden; Thomaston, on Route 1 just west of Rockland; and Castine, on Route 175 south from Route 1 just east of Bucksport. Route 1 through Tomaston passes an impressive array of very large homes of the past, and the street itself makes an interesting photographic subject.

On Route 1, just east of Bath, at Wiscasset, there are some fine old homes (a couple are open to the public and cameras are welcome), and although the harbor is not overly busy, it does contain the frequently photographed schooner wrecks, *Luther Little* and *Hesper*, abandoned close to Route 1 bridge in 1935 and still intact at this writing.

Much farther eastward, there are the more austere coastal towns of Jonesport, at the end of Route 187, off Route 1 at Columbia Falls, Lubec, at the end of Route 189 off Route 1 at Whiting, and Eastport, at the end of Route 190, off Route 1 at Perry, the latter two being the easternmost communities in the United States. It's a long way out and around a couple of bays, but don't miss Eastport if you like old towns that smack of the sea and the past. There are hilltop neighborhoods in Eastport where stark old houses

Don't miss Eastport if you like old towns that smack of the sea and the past.

stand like sentinels with long sea views behind and before them, and there's a thoroughly weather-beaten row of waterfront wharves, where 17-foot tides cause unusual docking problems. Eastport has had its unhappy days, beset with economic adversity for many of its years, but has recently been enjoying the beginnings of "rediscovery."

Brunswick, on Route 1, 20 miles east of Portland, is a handsome old college town with a goodly number of old houses, although it has grown recently as a business community. The attractive campus of Bowdoin College harbors many fine examples of college architecture and at least one ivied hall that dates far back into the past.

For a lively, busy summer town, with much human activity on both shore and water, visit Boothbay Harbor on Route 27 from Route 1 as you leave Wiscasset eastward. It has every colorful aspect of the tourist scene from oceangoing fishing vessels to visiting yachts and schooners to those narrow little streets filled with picturesque gift shops and eating places. A long narrow public footbridge crosses an inter portion of the deep blue harbor, affording numerous, ever-changing picture possibilities. Don't neglect the drive out Route 27 to Southport. Here one blue cove after another greets the eye, their steep wooded shores dotted with scattered white cottages — you've seen artists' impressions of them in many a watercolor. At the tip end of 27 is Newagen, with lobster wharves and an interesting view toward semidistant Cuckold Lighthouse, serene on its lonely island.

Rockport, on Route 1 between Camden and Rockland, on Penobscot Bay, is an attractive old village built on low hills that overlook a deep and pleasant harbor. It is one of the few coastal towns where parks and homes, rather than commercial buildings, border the shore. There are three parks on Rockport's waterfront — four if you regard the public landing as one. There is parking space at the water's edge and much space to stroll about with a camera. Two cruise schooners berth at Rockport, and numerous other craft are often tied at moorings or landings.

Camden, adjoining Rockport, on Route 1, is an attractive and busy town, well-liked by travelers. It boasts one of the most photogenic harbors on the Maine coast, a harbor that in summer is almost ridiculously busy for its size, with cruise schooners, yachts, lobster boats, small pleasure craft, and excursion boats often trying to navigate at once. There are many vantage points for pictures here, and when cameras are pointed in an inland direction across the

Boothbay Harbor has every colorful aspect of the tourist scene.

CAMDEN, MAINE. harbor, rocky Mount Battie forms a strong background.

A number of the Maine coast cruising schooners have made Camden their home port for many years. They can be easily photographed from various locations, especially from the attractive little park that faces the whole harbor like a theater balcony, with high sloping lawns and curving walks. Shots of the harbor and schooners, taken from these lawns, have adorned calendars and restaurant walls for years. Between the park and the public landing, the Megunticook River pours into the harbor, creating an attractive waterfall and rapids when water is high.

At Camden's public landing, there are lines of benches where people sit for hours watching the ever-moving harbor scene. Here you may photograph schooners, work boats, dinghies, and other craft from every conceivable angle and close enough to touch. For the schooners, be on hand during the weekend, for they are at sea the rest of the week, departing one by one on Monday mornings. The departures themselves are photogenic, whether you catch them at the

CAMDEN HARBOR.

landing with people on board and on shore waving goodbye, or as they pass close to the Camden Yacht Club in the west channel or close to the boat repair wharves on the east side. The schooners leave the inner harbor pushed or pulled by motorboats, so don't expect full-sail close-ups. You can catch them in full sail when they put on canvas in the outer harbor, either by telephoto lens or by taking the harbor sightseeing crafts at the right time.

The schooners chiefly face northwest when they're moored in the harbor, so if you want sun on the bows, let the late afternoon sun swing well to the west before shooting. Misty, pearly sunrise shots with masts silhouetted against brilliant cream and gold have sometimes been effectively obtained. There are even possibilities under a full moon. I once photographed the harbor at 10:00 P.M. from a tripod in the park, catching the moon just over a schooner's mainmast, with both moon and shore lights casting light streamers on the water. (Don't begrudge the shore lights at times like this; they'll prove that your picture is a night shot rather than a sunlight exposure darkly printed!)

Maine's cruise schooners have appeared in a number of motion pictures, including *Captains Courageous* in 1977, when Camden's harbor experienced a storm at sea, artificially created with wind and wave machines and filmed at 2:00 A.M. with some carefully placed lights). The final scene filmed was the arrival of the schooner *Adventure*, repainted to represent the fictional *We're Here*. Local Camden people, enjoying themselves as extras, roamed the landing in period clothing, while all cars and modern boats were banished from sight. As the schooner came in and cameras rolled, traffic was halted on Route 1, lest a car stray within range of a lens.

Rockland, the chief commercial city on Maine's midcoast, is by no means purely a shopping and fish-packing center. The harbor has been very much "spruced up" in recent years, and now picturesquely hosts shore restaurants and a growing number of cruise schooners. The annual early August Lobster Festival, held here at harborside, is a major event and can provide a wealth of colorful human interest photographs — anything from bands on parade, beauty queens, and harbor activities to a thousand or more people dining at one time.

Just east of Bucksport, Route 1 affords access to a tranquil territory, much loved by those who, for artistic, retirement, or vacation reasons, have sought an unhurried, off-the-beaten-path location. It is part farm country and part tidal boating and fishing country, where rural barns can be a stone's throw from a commercial fishermen's wharf. The roads here wind through pleasant little communities, around and across inlets, and in general reveal much scenic charm worthy of the camera.

STONINGTON.

Turn south into Route 15 from Route 1 at Orland to enter this picturesque area. Orland itself is an attractive village with a white, lawn-surrounded church, often photographed across the peaceful Narramissic River. Blue Hill, a favorite of many in this area, is the next community of any size you'll reach — a village of nice old homes, some historic, facing a quiet cove.

Continue along Route 15 and you'll reach similarly attractive Brooksville, Little Deer Isle, Deer Isle, and eventually the old port of Stonington. A long, narrow inlet know by the Alice-in-Wonderland name Eggemoggin Reach, separates the Deer Isles from the mainland. You can find a number of interesting fishing and boating subjects to photograph here, ranging from power craft to loberstering scenes. The highway bridge across Eggemoggin Reach is an interesting central object itself. At Blue Harbor you can follow a little side road to Brooklin, which is a center for small boating activity at the east end of the Reach, much admired by those who build, repair, sail, and dream wooden boats. No excuse here for not getting a good boat shot, even of a boatbuilder at work.

Forts

FORT KNOX SEEMS to have been built for photographing — not the Kentucky Fort Knox where all the gold is, but a big intact 19th-century Maine fort on the Penobscot River near Bucksport. It's just off Route 1 as you approach the Waldo-Hancock Bridge heading east. Many people are surprised at what they find here: a complete granite-blocked fort with an inner court, stone stairways, cannons, dungeonlike inner rooms, and a commanding view of the river. It's a hugh stage set; a world of its own in a time of its own, and of course it's all historically real, having once been a commissioned United States Army fort, with not a stone replaced. There are picture scenes galore here, indoors and outdoors, from stone parapets, through granite archways, or from outdoor ledges.

At Edgecomb, just southward off Route 1 east of Wiscasset, there's an octagonal 1807 wooden fort that's a favorite for photographers. Fort Edgecomb stands simply and alone in the center of a broad lawn, with grassy terraces leading down to the shore of a quiet bay.

Fort McClary, on Route 103 just outside Kittery (the first town you come to as you enter the state on I-95 or Route 1), makes an interesting photo subject with

FORT KNOX. its hexagonal form. Atop a steep knoll, it is not easy to photograph well, but the many angles and possibilities should intrigue you. It has been rebuilt in part many times and its literal age is difficult to determine, but it was garrisoned in five wars, from the Revolution to World War I.

Mountain Tops

MOUNTAIN SUMMITS make good scenic spots, and there are two on the coast that can be reached by car on paved roads. Cadillac Mountain, in Acadia National Park, is the highest — a solid dome of bald rock rising behind Bar Harbor like a stone elephant. At its 1,500-foot summit there's a varied view of ocean, bay, scores of islands, and the rumpled expanse of the mainland. The road is gradual and maintained in excellent shape.

Mount Battie, in Camden, is only 700 feet high, but the view from it is superb, in that a number of hills, bays, lakes, coves, highways, and towns are visible at once in an interesting tapestry. You can climb a stone tower here, but it's not really necessary, as the mountain's broad, bald summit offers many unobstructed vantage points for panoramic views. The entrance to

FORT EDGECOMBE.

Mount Battie's toll road is on Route 1, one mile north of Camden.

Other high hills in the Camden area may be climbed easily on hiking trails, notably 1,300-foot Mount Megunticook. Ragged Mountain, just west of Camden, has a ski lift (Camden Snow Bowl), and the view in winter of blue sea and white mountains is well worth the ascent even if you're not a skier.

Blueberry Barrens

IF YOU WANT something with mood and an elusive ingredient to capture on film, try the great blueberry barrens of Washington County, Maine's huge eastern-most county, larger than Rhode Island, and traversed chiefly by Routes 1 and 9. You have to see to believe the slightly rolling, rock-strewn plains that spread to the far horizon with a hardy ground cover of pure blueberry all the way. The barrens begin at Cherryfield, extending inland and eastward for many miles. Take Route 193 northward from Route 1 out of Cherryfield, or Route 192 northward from Route 1 out of Machias, and you'll drive through portions of them. There's a rough loneliness to the barrens, as on the moors of Scotland and the Cornish coast of England — but if you'd prefer more life, come in mid-August, when the barrens are swarming with berry pickers.

If you want something with mood, try the great blueberry barrens of Washington County.

Scenic Routes

THERE ARE MANY off-trail roads in Maine that will lead you to photogenic scenes, chiefly roads that head for the sea, such as Route 32 out of Waldoboro to Pemaquid, with its vistas of broad bays across the downward curving fields of old farms, or Route 92 as it winds along a sheltered but salty shoreline from Machias down through Machiasport and beyond. There's a big, handsome old church at Machiasport, standing dramatically on a knoll with the sea behind it — a fine photographic subject even when it's cloudy and the offshore inlets are half-buried in rolling mist.

Follow Route 24 out of Brunswick and you'll eventually find yourself on the ridge of a narrow peninsula that thins and then breaks, into Bailey and Orrs Islands. The road bridges from island to island, dipping and curving between steep little rocky coves and high-perched cottages — the sort of distilled New England coastal scene often seen in watercolors on Christmas cards.

Route 15 winds its ways seaward from Orland to Blue Hill, Sedgewick, Deer Isle, and eventually Stonington, through a collection of attractive little communities, half marine, half inland rural. Stonington is a long way from Route 1, but it's an old handsome fishing and boatbuilding town, filled with structures of a bygone seaside era.

Farther eastward, Route 191 skirts the lonely shore of Washington County out of East Machias, touching the little harbor of Cutler, often photographed for its pure, unblemished sampling of traditional Maine coast atmosphere.

NARRAGAUGUS BAY.

The roads through and around Acadia National Park abound with scenic possibilities, especially since you can park in so many places and hike easily to various vantage points. Farther west and a bit inland, Route 235 between Waldoboro and Hope follows high ridges with views of lakes, orchards, and hills that roll serenely off into the distance; this route is particularly attractive in autumn.

Maine roads have a scenic advantage over those in many other areas of the country, in that they tend to follow the hilltops rather than the stream valleys. Many a Maine road, rather than lead you through heavy riverside vegetation, will take you to meadowed hilltops with sweeping views.

The Islands

DON'T NEGLECT THE islands off the Maine coast or dismiss them as a handful of lonely lumps in a storm-tossed sea. There are hundreds of them, many of

THE PUBLIC LANDING, MONHEGAN.

them inviting rather than forbidding, and a great number can easily be visited by boat, or even by car. They range from small meadowed islets with wild-flowers and white cottages, to hilly sprawling islands complete with old lighthouses and lobstering ports. A few are barren, with ghostly rock formations; others, thick with evergreens, stand like hair brushes on the horizon — uninhabited, perhaps, but admired and often explored by cruising boaters.

Ten miles off the tip of Pemaquid Point lies enchanting old **Monhegan**, certainly the Maine island that best fits the classic notion of what such an island should be — rugged, wooded, with surf pounding its lonely shores on the east and a rustic fishing community hugging its tiny sheltered harbor on the west.

Reached by ferry from Port Clyde year-round and by summer excursions from Boothbay Harbor and sometimes New Harbor, Monhegan is still small enough to be covered in a one-day visit if you don't mind plenty of walking. (You must leave your car at a dockside parking field on the mainland.)

Monhegan's small but colorful village is loaded with character and charm. Along the rock-rimmed harbor, fishermen's houses stand on the steep slopes, lobster traps piled high in backyards, and boats are often moored to jagged rocks. Farther up the slope, the smaller inland houses often resemble cottages in Mother Goose illustrations — neat and plain, with tiny gardens or picket fences close around them.

As the dirt paths and narrow streets climb ever higher on the steep hillside, incredible sea views unfold, and you can often shoot deep blue harbor and ocean with the gabled edges of houses in the foreground and a meadow that curves downward out of sight. When fog clouds race through, or a thick mistiness lurks over the harbor, there are many challenging creative picture possibilities.

Monhegan's lighthouse stands at the center of the island, on its highest point. From the lighthouse grounds there are excellent panorama views of the village, its fjordlike harbor, and the barren island of Manana, which rises just across the harbor like a chunk of the moon. The mainland, when it is visible, is a thin gray line along the horizon.

Monhegan's small but colorful village is loaded with character and charm.

Beyond the lighthouse, the paths take to the woods, but you're not in a vast forest. Before many steps you can often hear the muted booming of surf ahead. The path ends abruptly and perhaps startlingly at a high clifftop, with the Atlantic surf far below you and the unbroken ocean ahead. On a wide trail you can stroll along the clifftops here for a mile or more with not a house, dock, or even a printed sign in sight; just an occasional artist painting at his easel, or a few vacationers propped against a rock in the sun, reading.

There are other islands: large ones, such as **Isle au Haut**, reached by ferry from Stonington, where Route 15 ends; **Swans Island**, reached by ferry from Bass Harbor, where Route 102 ends on Mount Desert Island; and **Vinalhaven**, **North Haven**, and **Islesboro**, visitable by regular ferry service. The Islesboro ferry, from Route 15 at Lincolnville, and the ferries to Vinalhaven and North Haven from the Terminal on Route 1 at Rockland, carry cars. You may find much to photograph from the Rockland ferries themselves as they wind between small islands and pass within waving distance of most anything from a cruising yacht to a child on shore. Vinalhaven, once the home of large granite quarries, is a sprawling island with rambling cottage-lined roads and a sturdily built old village with its main street facing the harbor.

Wherever you go, keep your eyes open. Everyone sees something different to photograph on the Maine coast: an ancient well pump or hitching post; a flow-

MOOSELOOKMEGUNTIC LAKE.

er-potted lamppost; freshly caught fish on sale at wharfside or on open decks; or a boat owner painting his hull at low tide on a muddy shore. The "little things" are varied and everywhere.

Inland Maine

The Western Lakes

UMBAGOG, MOOSELOOKMEGUNTIC, Kennebago, Aziscoos, (or Azischos), — the old Abenaki Indian names roll enchantingly out of the north woods. They are names of lakes of the Rangeley Lake region; not "tame" lakes as in city parks, but grand sweeps of deep water bordered by rough forests and backed by misty mountain peaks. Some are as long as 15 miles, and when strong winds blow, real surf crashes roughly on their rocky shores. And when it's quiet at evening, fish jump on the calming surfaces and the sad cry of the loon may be heard across the water.

Yet, near-wilderness though this region may be, modern highways reach in, scattered cabins number in the many hundreds, camps and motels are present, and there are several excellent motorhome campgrounds. Hiking trails criss-cross through the forest and wind up the mountain slopes to scenic vistas, waterfalls, and hidden ponds. Chair lifts to high summits carry skiers in winter and view-seekers in summer. The region is wild, beautiful, and spacious, but only a couple of hours drive from the Maine coast or from the White Mountains of New Hampshire. It is well worth a long visit with your camera if you enjoy photographing nature and the outdoors without sugar coating.

The homeland of the Abenaki Indians until the American Revolution, the Rangeley Lakes were not settled until the 1790s, and from then on but scantily for many decades. During the late 1800s the region became logging country, and in the 1920s was first made available to a vacationing public, primarily to those who loved fishing. The tracks of an old logging railroad brought special fishing trains from as far

MOOSELOOKMEGUNTIC LAKE.

away as New York City, as exciting reports of huge trout and other fish circulated.

The logging railroad is gone now, replaced by modern highways, and facilities for many outdoor activities have been developed, though never in a congested "resort complex" sense. Wherever you go, wherever you pause, there is always an unmistakable realization that the true north woods are at hand.

Fishing is still a major feature. The lakes are regularly stocked with trout and salmon, and many a city escapee sets out at dawn or sunset in a small boat with a low horsepower engine and fishing line ready. Fishing is reported best between ice-out in May and the end of June, but whether or not a large number of fish are caught is sometimes immaterial. If you're both a fisherman and a photographer, by all means get out on the water. There is perhaps nothing so restful to the spirit as to sit in a gently drifting boat with a colorful sunset before you, miles of open lake around you, and distant pine-clad mountains rising in diffused mystery.

The best known and most utilized of the Rangeley Lakes are Mooselookmeguntic (you're not required to call it anything more than "Mooselook" these days) and Rangeley. Mooselook is the big fellow, 15 miles long and 7 miles wide at the center, its shores heavily wooded. It provides photographers with some of the most definitive and photogenic north woods subject matter in New England. Even its shoreline stacks of weather-whitened driftwood branches, deposited there when the lake was expanded a few decades ago, make prime creative photo subjects as well as home decorative articles.

For a grand scenic vista, called by some photographers the finest panoramic shot in Maine, follow Route 17 south from Oquossoc and up to the high mountain pass known as Height-of-Land. This vantage point offers wide and far-reaching views of mountains and lakes, dominated by the expanse of Mooselook, looking very much as though mankind had never touched it.

The lake's chief service village is Oquossoc, where Route 4 ends and Route 17 begins. There are fine views from here westward over Mooselook, as well as one of the state's best calendar shots, eastward over Rangeley Lake.

For good views on the lake shore, visit Bugle Cove, just south of Oquossoc, or Bemis, at the lake's southern end, where the 1920s rail line ended and a large rustic fishing camp once sprawled. The Bemis

Road, following an old rail route of Oquossoc, will take you to these shore points. Westerly winds prevail very strongly across Mooselook, and at times surprisingly rough surf will crash on the stony strand of the east shore, adding much interesting action to your shore shots.

If you'd like to continue to combine photography with hiking, we don't hesitate to suggest 2,200-foot Bald Mountain, at Oquossoc. The trail here will give you magnificent views of both Rangeley and Mooselookmeguntic Lake.

Rangeley Lake, although only a bit smaller than Mooselook, always seems a bit less turbulent than its big sister to the west. Its shores are less wild and primitive in appearance. It is bordered for about half its length by meadows and lawns, by a number of camps and motels, and even a golf course, but it still has plenty of photogenic vantage points. Saddleback Mountain, topping 4,000 feet and the highest in the region, adds a strong scenic touch at the lake's eastern end. Capture it with a telephoto lens as you

GREENVALE COVE, RANGELEY LAKE.

RANGELEY LAKE.   approach Rangeley village from the west on Route 4/16 — from here you can get a nice strong highway and mountainous shot.

You can drive all the way around Rangeley Lake on paved roads — 25 miles all told — by way of Oquossoc and Rangeley State Park. The latter, on the lake's wooded south shore, contains an attractive beach, open lawns, and many facilities for enjoying the lake and forest. There are opportunities for sailing and watersport shots with scenic backgrounds.

The most scenic views of Rangeley Lake, from the standpoint of being easy to catch with a camera, are at the outlet overpass off Route 16 immediately east of Oquossoc, and on Route 4 at Dallas Hill, south of Rangeley village. The latter spot is a high point on the highway, just above the lake's eastern end, where you can obtain an unobstructed view of the entire lake with island, bordering hills, and background mountains strongly visible.

Rangeley village, at the northeast corner of the lake, is a small but busy community — a friendly, informal town with a main street of gift shops, banks, churches, small restaurants, and supply stores for the outdoors enthusiast. There is a touch of Western Frontier heartiness here.

The third lake of the Rangeley chain, counting

"backward" from east to west (but downstream as the outlets go), is Richardson, 17 miles long, though quite narrow, and probably the most secluded and wilderness-touched of the big lakes. The only way to reach the camping and service end of Richardson Lake by car is to follow Route 5, which begins on Route 2 just west of Rumford and winds its way northward through rural Andover into the forested mountains — a paved but lovely, lonely road.

This route dead-ends at the lake, and although there are excellent camping facilities here for RVs, there are few other aspects of civilization for many miles. Stand on the shore here and 17 miles of deep lake curve out of sight into forested mountains before you. A local sign advises, "All wilderness sites reached by boat or canoe only."

The northern tip of Richardson Lake is close to Route 16, though out of sight from that highway. An access road has recently been cut through the woods here to a boat launching site. Just below its midpoint, Richardson Lake outflows to Umbagog Lake through the Rapid River, a location familiar to fans of author Louise Dickinson Rich, who wrote of her experiences here in *We Took to the Woods*.

Farther westward, Umbagog, another of the larger Rangeley Lakes, sprawls across the border into New Hampshire. Umbagog Lake is not as deep as the other lakes, and being a bit far from the Rangeley scene, is not as actively caught up in the boating and fishing activities generated for tourists. As a result, it is much less used and has fewer cottages and landings on its shores, making it excellent for nature and wildlife photography, but short on watersports and human interest scenes.

North of Umbagog Lake, the fifth Rangeley Lake, Aziscoos, reaches far into steep and forested mountains. Completely created within the valley of the Megalloway River by the husky dam at Wilsons Mills early in this century, it is still a new lake with rough, irregular shores. Hunting and fishing camps have only recently been established on its shores. The wild cascade of the liberated Megalloway waters below the Wilson Mills dam can be photographed easily from Route 16.

All of the Rangeley Lakes are part of the headwaters of the Androscoggin River, which begins where the Megalloway River merges with the outlet of Umbagog Lake, a few miles south of Wilsons Mills. The Androscoggin then wanders through northern New Hampshire and western Maine to eventually join the Kennebec River near the coast.

Kennabago is one of those lakes that have an air of silent north woods mystery about them.

There are scores of small lakes in the Rangeley region, some deep in forest and reachable only by trail, others at the ends of narrow backroads. If you'd like to photograph a small lake closely bordered by steep mountain slopes and dark pine forest, try Kennebago Lake, at the end of the Lincoln Pond Road, 10 miles or so north of Rangeley village. Reach Lincoln Pond Road by following the Morton cut-off from Route 4. Kennabago is one of those lakes that have an air of silent north woods mystery about them, particularly on late summer mornings when thick rising mists catch the early sunlight. Trails into the forest here are not tame paths in park woods; they'll convince you that the Three Bears are just past the next boulder. Those who visit cabins when snow is on the ground and observe the broad footprints will assure you they *are* close by, although you're not likely to see them.

The entire Rangeley region is a paradise for hikers, and if you care to take your camera on a rugged hike for scenic mountain and deep forest shots, inquire locally at Rangeley or Oquossoc. There are novice mountain climbing routes up Bald and Spotted Mountains, and there's a trail south of Rangeley village that will take you to a couple of hidden waterfalls and a striking rocky outcrop known as Piazza Rock.

The area is in fact criss-crossed with trails, but most of them will entail the equivalent of a strenuous hike, and preparations are necessary. These are not paths thought nicely cleared woods, but wild routes that go long distances without road contact. They will sometimes cut steeply upward to cross rocky mountain shoulders, or may lead you to rushing streams that must be crossed with care. Local camping stores carry geodesic survey maps of the area. With their details of stream, trail, road, and shore they are of real value to the adventuring visitor.

If you envision photographing friends or others frolicking in water, summer swimming may prove a bit chilly in the big lakes, which resist warming with their great depth. The smaller lakes warm up nicely, though even in Rangeley's comparatively cool summer, so that water play is by no means complete absent.

Inland Maine, geared more to lumbering and farming, rather than to fishing, boatbuilding, and the busy commerce of the sea, grew more slowly than the coast. You'll find large towns farther apart and the land more thinly settled.

Most of what mankind has accomplished in inland Maine is clustered along the Kennebec and Penobscot Rivers.

The Kennebec and The Penobscot

THE LARGER COMMUNITIES and historic spots in inland Maine are chiefly on the rivers. The two great rivers of Maine, the Kennebec and the Penobscot, roughly divide the state into three sectors, not only geographically but in the human sense. The late Kenneth Roberts liked to say that you did not really enter Maine until you crossed the Kennebec. He viewed the region west of the Kennebec as more like the established countrysides of Massachusetts; less imbued with the lingering frontier flavor that had made Maine different. Although the last few decades have brought much growth and change, it is still true enough that east of the Kennebec you'll find more that is typical early Maine; less that could be anywhere in New England. Continuing northward and eastward beyond the Penobscot, you go one step farther into the past and into the realm of nature, with forests overpowering small villages that have thus far resisted great change. Most of what mankind has accomplished in inland Maine is clustered along the Kennebec and Penobscot Rivers. There's Augusta, the

MAINE STATE CAPITOL IN AUGUSTA.

state capital, for instance, 56 miles north of Portland and a little more than 100 miles from the New Hampshire border, reached very directly by both I-95 and the Maine Turnpike. If you enjoy photographing state capital buildings and the public monuments and edifices that usually accompany them, Augusta, though small as state capitals go, provides its share of architectural interest. The imposing capitol building itself, on State Street, designed by Charles Bullfinch, is just difficult enough to photograph to make it a

challenging subject. It stands on an upward slope
with a busy avenue and a low mall before it. Rather
than tip your camera upward, back across the
avenue, down into the mall, and then far out onto
the mall. A wide-angle lens is very useful here.

Elsewhere in Augusta, there are some fine old
houses, two or three of them immediately adjacent to
the capitol building, on State Street, including the
Executive Mansion, Blaine House. The bridge across
the Kennebec River provides a nice scenic view of
the downtown area.

When you leave Augusta in any direction, you
quickly enter a rural realm. Many of the smaller
towns here contain subjects of photographic interest,
especially in the genre of old streets and houses bordering lakes and streams. West of Augusta, you may
find Readfield, on Route 41, and Wayne, on Route
219, particularly photogenic in this respect, Wayne
actually has a lake on each side of its lower village,
so that half the houses in town are blessed with
backyard water frontage.

The Belgrade Lakes on Route 27, north of Augusta,
though more prim and tame in appearance than the

THE UNION FAIR.

Rangeley Lakes, provide many interesting lake and woodland views. Old lakefront homes here suggest the canoe and croquet vacations of decades ago. We've seen some beautiful sunsets here from the village landing, which faces westward across the water.

Gardner, just south of Augusta, on Route 201, has become a busy commercial center, but still boasts a handsome town square and numerous fine old beautifully maintained houses of grand proportion. At Skowhegan, farther up the Kennebec, at the Scott Paper Company, you'll have an opportunity to photograph paper-making machinery in action.

Farther eastward, a trip inland up the Penobscot River will provide perhaps more natural beauty than the Kennebec, but its shores also have their share of interesting communities. Bangor is a rugged city with many reflections and echoes of the past century, when it was for a time the lumber capital of the world. In the middle and late 1800s, steady parades of schooners and streamers carried an enormous volume of lumber down the Penobscot from Bangor to the sea. If you like to photograph unusual statues, there's a 30-foot statue of Paul Bunyan on the Route 1 approach to Bangor and a towering 65-foot Indian statue at Skowhegan, on Route 201 north of Waterville, handcarved by the late Bernard Langlois.

North of Bangor, Old Town, on Route 2 or via I-95, still carries on some of the old lumbering trade, and between it and its sister city of Orono, the sprawling campus of the growing University of Maine provides a photogenic subject.

The Maine Forest and Logging Museum, at this writing still under construction on Route 178 at Bradley (north of Bangor), should prove a fascinating collection of photographic subjects for all who are intrigued by logging camps, sawmill machinery, and all that goes with the forest-to-lumber field of effort. An entire mill will be a major part of the complex, due for completion some time in 1991. Should you be further interested in photographing reminders of logging days, you might like the intact remains of an elaborate tramway that once carried logs over land from one waterway to another. This is at Eagle Lake, just south of Fort Kent on Route 11 — an Aroostook County location that we mention here because of its tie-in with the Logging Museum.

Still farther north, on Route 15, north of Bangor, Dover-Foxcroft is an interesting mixture of old established New England town and rustic farm community. It has one of the more interesting church steeples found this far from the large cities. Drive northward

toward Moosehead Lake from here on Route 15, and the little village of Monson will provide some spectacular views of mountains and farm valley.

AN OLD MAINE DOORWAY.

Moosehead Lake and the Northern Wilderness

The forested areas around Moosehead Lake provide one of the best opportunities in Maine to see and photograph moose.

MOOSEHEAD LAKE, on Route 15, the largest lake in Maine, is like the Rangeley Lakes in many respects, though it is all one big lake. The forests here seem just a bit deeper, the bears perhaps a bit closer, and the shores a bit wilder. Paper companies own much of the shore here, and there are few camps and cottages. The service town for the lake, Greenville, on Route 6, north of Guilford, is at the lower end, as are most of the camps and tourist spots. The best and most accessible views for cameras on Moosehead's shores are no doubt on Route 6, which follows the shore between Greenville and Moosehead village. The shot everybody takes is the view of Mount Kineo, seen across water on its rocky island. In some places you can capture it with groves of shore pines or birches in the foreground.

The 75-year-old steamboat *Katahdin*, which once afforded passengers excellent opportunities to photograph Mount Kineo and other Moosehead Lake sights, no longer makes excursions. But restored to its prime condition, it serves as a very interesting and photogenic exhibit at the Moosehead Marine Museum in Greenville.

Just off Route 11 east of Greenville, there is another unusual subject that you might find of photographic interest: the Katahdin Iron Works, where the remains of a blast furnace and its accompanying kiln mark the ghostly remnants of an 1880 iron works that actually thrived in the seeming wilderness.

And regarding the wilderness, the forested areas around Moosehead Lake provide one of the best opportunities in Maine to see and photograph moose. They are scattered and unpredictable of course, but unlike bears, they make no attempt to keep clear of humans and vehicles — one might surprise you by sauntering out into the highway.

East of Moosehead Lake, the mountains become high again, with Baxter State Park surrounding the highest of their group: 5,268-foot Mount Katahdin, which, after the Presidential Range in the White Mountains, is the highest summit in New England. Rugged and cliffsided, Katahdin rises imposingly as a more or less solitary peak, having very few foothills or rangelike links to other mountains. There are many places to capture it on film as you approach, and its hugh pile of cliffs and domed shoulders will look a bit different in each season, from each angle, and whenever the light changes.

As with other very high elevations, Mount Katahdin should be climbed only with proper hiking gear and with park ranger approval. But if you do make the ascent, there is much in the way of rugged scenic interest to photograph. Trails are well marked on the mountain, which is the northern terminus of the Appalachian Trail.

Beyond Katahdin the forest wilderness reaches on and on to the Canadian border in a thoroughly wild stretch penetrated chiefly by lumber tractors, loggers, trappers, and occasional whitewater canoe parties. The Allagash, just north of Mount Katahdin, is one of the least tamed forest areas in the eastern United States, and access roads are closed except to those well-equipped and experienced hikers who have received a permit from the Maine Department of Conservation.

At the far eastern side of Maine, the forest comes to a broken edge and the landscape takes on a mid-western or even western plains appearance. This is the Aroostook countryside, which extends along the New Brunswick border to the northern tip of the state. Small towns here are surrounded by large, flat farms, many of them growing the Maine potatoes that have long reached the nation's food markets — and if you don't think potato blossoms are worthy of color photography, just catch a mile-long field of them in bloom!

Although the Aroostook area of extreme northern Maine does not have the abundance of typically New England subject matter so prevalent southward (some have even commented that a touch of the Dakotas prevails here), there is no absence of photogenic material.

The most rapid way to reach this region is to take I-95 from Bangor northward to its terminus at Houlton. But a much more interesting way, from the photographic point of view, is to stick to good old Route 1. After traversing Maine's Atlantic coast, Route 1 swings northward in the Eastport area and follows the St. Croix and St. John River valleys, along with the Canadian border, to the upper tip of the state.

At Calais, through which Route 1 will take you, there are a number of delightful river views with a different flavor: the broad St. Croix as wide as a large lake in some spots, twisting as a mountain creek at others, and with the Canadian shore just across the way. St. Stephen, New Brunswick, is but a short bridge crossing from Calais, should you wish to make an international jaunt. Calais itself (pronounced "Callus" by the way, not like its namesake in France) has a number of attractive old neighborhoods, especially in its Main Street Historic District, which has some interesting Victorian Gothic architecture. If you're in the vicinity in August, events at the week-long International Festival should provide colorful costume, parade, and special event subject material.

Heading northward from Calais on Route 1 you're still in Washington County until you pass Danforth at the Aroostook County line, but all of this territory is a beautifully wild and remote region of heavy forest, wilderness lakes, and rising hills. If you'd like a chance for mood shots over lonely waters, with wild birds fluttering noisily upward or a morning mist in the air, you can reach the shore of broad Baskahegan Lake at Brookton or Crooked Brook Lake at Eaton. You don't have to leave Route 1 for more than a few yards to get to either one.

All of this territory is a beautifully wild and remote region of heavy forest, wilderness lakes, and rising hills.

The key places in Aroostook County for photographing are in the string of towns linked together by Route 1 as you near Maine's northern tip.

At Littleton, just north of Houlton, you'll find the northernmost covered bridge in New England, attractively spanning Medaxnekeag Stream. Leave Route 1 for just a couple of miles at Caribou, turning northward onto Route 161, and you soon reach New Sweden, where the local historical society maintains an eye-catching exhibit of authentic pioneer log cabins and artifacts of the early settlers. Here is excellent photographic potential in a true Maine north woods setting.

At Van Buren, where Route 1 reaches Maine's northern border, there's a re-creation of the settlement pioneered in the 1700s by the Acadians of *Evangeline* fame. This is one of those intriguing reconstructions that sets the imagination to work and can definitely provide numerous settings and angles for photographs.

At Fort Kent, you can feel that you've definitely driven to "the end of the line." Here Route 1 ends (or begins its long journey to Key West, Florida, if you'd rather look at it the other way). Route 161 goes a little farther, but tends to turn back southward. Fort Kent's fine old 1839 blockhouse, looking as though it had been built with huge new Lincoln Logs, makes a striking photographic subject on West Main Street.

NEW HAMPSHIRE

The White Mountains

The most concentrated display of scenic grandeur in New England probably lies in the White Mountains of New Hampshire, where a jumble of towering glacier-scarred heaps of granite have excited imaginations since colonial days — and have certainly lured photographers in droves.

Unlike most high mountain regions, especially some of the long Appalachian ridges farther south, the White Mountains are not barriers to smooth vehicular travel. Highways don't climb slowly up one side of a ridge and down the other. These mountains are broken through by deep valleys. You can drive through the heart of them on smooth roads in a couple of hours if you wish, although you might linger for weeks and not see all the scenic highlights.

There is virtually every type of New England photographic subject in the White Mountains: the majesty of high peaks, scenic lakes and ponds; handsome waterfalls; covered bridges; towering cliffs; and picturesque villages.

THE WHITE MOUNTAINS
FROM I-95 NEAR FRANCONIA.

Mountain Grandeur

KEY SCENIC FEATURES worth photographing may be found on any of four routes through the mountains. Route 302, curving down through Crawford Notch, and I-93, sweeping through Franconia Notch, will show you the richest of the high mountain scenery. Route 16, farther east, will give you the best views of Mount Washington, and the east-west Kancamagus Highway (part of Route 112) will show you some magnificent high mountain stretches of forested wilderness. A number of specific places are worth calling to attention.

Mount Washington The big fellow, its 6,288-foot summit the highest in the northeastern United States, is taller than the others by just enough to poke its top into what is virtually a different climate zone. It reaches up into a zone of high winds, often cold and abruptly violent, and often very different from prevailing weather on lower summits. Hence Mount Washington's unfortunate history of having killed a good many people. It has tossed hikers off cliffs with hurricane gusts on mild spring days, rendered them hopelessly lost in blinding October snow, and set world wind velocity records (232 miles per hour) at its specially constructed summit weather stations. The peak's encounter with cold air currents also accounts for another of its drawbacks — the fact that a cloud often forms or lingers at the summit, harming both the view from the top and views of the summit itself from the valley.

It's a tough mountain to photograph, and although we certainly don't want to steer anyone away from it, its summit is more often buried in cloud than any tourist promoter would dare admit. But — and this is a very important "but" — the mountain often looks impressive in a wild and mysterious way when its summit is buried in dark cloud. The lower portions that remain visible always appear majestic, the ponderous shoulders seeming to include enough granite to make half a dozen additional mountains. Mount Washington actually looks bigger when its summit is hidden.

In any event, you can get your best or certainly handiest shots of Mount Washington from the lawn or picnic park at Glen House on Route 16, about nine miles south of Gorham (or 16 miles north of North Conway). Several of the other high peaks are also visible from here, ranging to the right of Mount Washington. Here's where the road to the summit

The mountain often looks impressive in a wild and mysterious way when its summit is buried in dark cloud.

begins, and if the summit is free of clouds when you arrive, we recommend by all means that you go to the top. There's a coach bus to the summit if you're hesitant about driving yourself, and if the road is open to the public, don't worry about violent weather: forestry and state park officials watch the weather situation pretty closely. In fact, at the bus ticket office you can read indicators showing the temperature and wind velocity at the summit.

On the west side of the mountain (the opposite side as you look from Glen House), the colorful old Cog Railway, built in 1869, makes its climb to the top, slanting up the bare upper slopes at a 37-degree incline like a misplaced toy train. You can reach the beginning of the Cog Railway at the end of a well-indicated side road that turns off Route 302 at

SACO RIVER DAM AT WILLEY POND, CRAWFORD NOTCH.

Fabyan, just north of Bretton Woods. Here too, you can get good close-up views of the mountain, and shots of or from the Cog cars are always interesting.

The Presidential Range Mount Washington is of course the highest peak in what has been called the Presidential Range — virtually one long, irregular mountain with a number of separate peaks, most of them named for presidents. This compact range tops 5,000 feet in at least seven separately named summits, making it the most pretentious array of peaks in the northeast.

It isn't easy to view and photograph the whole range, but we can think of one attractive spot that does the trick: the little high village of Sugar Hill, just west of Franconia. Climb to it on Route 117 out of

GLEN ELLIS FALLS, ROUTE 16 AT PINKHAM NOTCH.

Franconia and you'll find two or three places where the whole Presidential Range, plus nearer Mount Lafayette, is spectacularly in view. You can also see large portions of the range from Route 2 in the vicinity of Jefferson Highlands and from closer points on Route 16 near Glen House, such as the summit of Wildcat Mountain, which can be reached by gondola. For all its great bulk, the Presidential Range is elusive to photograph, because its own shoulders and foothills so often get in the way.

Mount Chocorua Don't say "Chocka-*rua*," say "Choc-*aur*ua." Some brochures have claimed that this mountain, with its Matterhorn profile, is the most photographed mountain in the eastern United States. Although experienced photographers tend to doubt this, it is quite probably photographed with frequency, because of its location. Situated just off Route 16 at a point where that highway enters the White Mountains, it is often the first high summit tourists see. It rises grandly across Chocorua Lake, where a large picnic area attracts many motorists and affords excellent birch shore vantage points. The park and lake, on Route 16 between West Ossippee and Conway, are pleasant and other interesting shots can be taken here.

Crawford Notch The drive through Crawford Notch on Route 302 will show you plenty of high mountains at close range. For its entire length, Crawford Notch is closely walled by mountains, and much of it is part of Crawford Notch State Park. The mountain closeness is particularly noticeable at Willey House, about halfway along the Notch Valley. Here there's a pond, a park area, a cafeteria, and a gift shop. Many travelers and most of the tour buses pause here for a stretch of the legs and a look around. The view of high mountains as seen across the pond is particularly impressive and is often photographed for publication. You can also shoot the towering 2,000-foot wall of Mount Webster, but the wall is so close you'll need a wide-angle lens if you don't want to tilt your camera upward.

Willey House is so named because it was here, in 1826, that two of the most severe avalanches in White Mountains history took place, each roaring straight at the unfortunate Willey family home, one from the front, the other from the rear. The first avalanche tore down from Mount Webster during spring rains, but stopped just short of the front of the little house after blocking the infant Saco River with rocks and debris. The second occurred during an August storm and roared down the mountain directly

THE NORTH CONWAY
SCENIC RAILWAY STATION.

behind the Willey home — a mountain understandably known today as Mount Willey. At the sound of the avalanche, the family apparently fled their home, possibly in panic. Tragically, although the house they left was unharmed, they themselves were fatally caught. The family dog, who somehow avoided getting caught in the slide, ran to the home of Mrs. Willey's father, Abel Crawford, who ran a trading post a few miles to the south. Big Abel Crawford, something of a legendary figure in White Mountains history, went back with the dog and discovered the tragedy.

The scars of both avalanches are still visible, especially the one on the steeper and more barren Mount Webster. There have been no severe slides since, but as you stand there in the little park and look up at the towering heights, it's easy to work up a bit of apprehension.

Franconia Notch This notch, on I-93, is also noted for photogenic mountains. One of them bears the famous craggy outthrust of rock that so strongly resembles a human face. This wonder, which has been known through the years as "The Old Man of the Mountain," "The Great Stone Face," and more recently as just "The Profile," is by no means hard to find. It is clearly visible from the highway, several hundred feet above the road, nigh enough to keep your neck craning as you draw close.

If you are approaching from the south, The Profile will be on your left. On the right at the same point, massive mountain shoulders rise steeply from the edge of the road itself. Part of one of the White Mountains' tallest peaks, Mount Lafayette, rises here, although you can't see its summit because you're a little too close under the bulging shoulders. This immediate stretch of highway provides a concentration of mountain scenery and high forested slopes that is probably the most compelling in the White Mountains.

The clearest and most "facelike" view of The Profile is from the shores of Echo Lake, which you will reach just ahead at the summit of the highway's long slow rise into the heart of the Notch. At the northern end of the lake there's a state park with ample parking space. For photographing The Profile, a telephoto lens is a must. The rocky outcrop is big enough to show as a face in a projected 35-millimeter slide, but without a telephoto lens, it will appear much too small in a 3½" x5" print. Echo Lake also offers many other mountain views and intriguing rock formations that are worthy of photographic attention — all the more if you take a tram ride to the summit of Cannon Mountain, the entrance to which is at the State Park Headquarters, beside Echo Lake.

The Kancamagus Highway affords some of the finest mountain vistas in the state.

Kancamagus Highway This portion of Route 112 links the Conways to the east with Lincoln and I-93 to the west. Originally a hiker's trail, the Kancamagus has no commercial or trading route history and, in fact, "takes the high road," following the high mountain shoulders rather than the valleys, although it does pursue the Swift River upward for a portion of its route. Traversing 35 miles of high-altitude wilderness, the Kancamagus Highway has no gas stations, eateries, or houses, but affords some of the finest mountain vistas in the state. Scenic turn-offs, picnic groves, campgrounds, and trails to waterfalls are frequent along the route, so there's always a place to get out and hike around a bit with your camera.

The Kancamagus Highway climbs to an altitude of 2,860 feet at its highest point, considered the highest elevation of any numbered highway in New England. But the road is wide, well-paved, and climbs gradually to this high point, and because there's so much to see at so many bends and pauses, you'll find it the shortest 35 miles you've ever driven. Be aware that this road is closed during snow season.

If you want a link between the southern end of

DIXVILLE NOTCH. Crawford Notch and the Kancamagus, try Bear Skin Notch Road, which comes down from the Kancamagus to the village of Bartlett. If you're coming up from Bartlett, you'll encounter some stiff climbs, but there are excellent view points. At one place, half of the peaks in the northern portion of the White Mountains, including Mount Washington, are visible.

OTHER MOUNTAIN VIEWING POINTS. A quiet side road that crosses the Saco River out of North Conway and skirts the edges of the mountains northward will take you to a rampart of tawny cliffs visible from Route 16. This is Cathedral Ledge, which adjoins Echo Lake State Park (not to be confused with Echo

Lake at Franconia Notch). When you get close to the cliffs you'll see a side road that will take you right under them and up and around to the summit. The view here — not only the mountain vistas, but the look straight down or along the edge of those dizzying cliffs — will delight anyone with a camera. You're protected by an iron railing, but leaning over that railing is like leaning out an upper window in a 70-story building.

The rock formations are intriguing, and if you're really lucky you might catch a mountain climber in training emerging via rope and piton. Alpine climbers often train here, and looking up from the foot of the cliffs, you can get excellent telephoto shots of them clinging to cliff faces like flies, groping carefully for each next safe step upward. Some people stand here entranced for hours, watching the climbers.

Should you wish to hike high into the mountains with your camera, the White Mountains are criss-crossed with more good trails than any other mountain area its size in the United States. A number of them, including the Appalachian Trail, intersect in the Franconia Notch area. To climb above 4,000 feet you must, of course, have hiking experience, be dressed correctly, and know what to expect on the higher slopes. Because of its well-prepared trails, Mount Lafayette is probably the easiest peak of its size to climb anywhere, but even this mountain has killed its share of hikers and cannot be taken lightly.

There is a one-track rail line that comes down through Crawford Notch, in some places clinging to the edges of the mountains. Until very recently, one freight train a day still chugged and puffed along this line. It's too late now to view moving trains, but at this writing the rails remain, and there is always the chance that some optimistic entrepreneur may install a sightseeing run of some kind. The old green Crawford Notch railroad station still stands near the head of the notch, presenting a nostalgic, photogenic scene. Beyond the head of the notch, railroad and highway proceed toward Littleton, passing through Bretton Woods, where one of the largest and most impressive summer hotels ever built still catches the eye.

Don't forget that the mountains north of Route 2 are also part of the White Mountains. They are not quite so high and not quite so interlaced with roads, trails, and places to visit, but nevertheless, afford a land of rugged, heavy-forested beauty. At Stark, on Route 110, are a covered bridge and white church that have appeared on many a calendar. A quiet vil-

The White Mountains are criss-crossed with more good trails than any other mountain area its size in the United States.

THE COLD RIVER,
SOUTH ACKWORTH.

lage surrounded by soaring forested slopes, Stark
doesn't see crowds of tourists but can be the central
point for rewarding hikes.

In the far northern reaches of the Whtie Mountains,
Route 26 climbs to 1,870-foot Dixville Notch, which
for about a half-mile presents a highly dramatic

mountain pass aspect. Twisting between steep cliffs, the road knifes through a high notch, sometimes into strong rushes of west wind, to emerge at a peaceful pond with a large, attractive resort hotel on its far side.

Southern New Hampshire

ALTHOUGH SOUTHERN New Hampshire lacks the spectacular mountain scenery of the northern region, it is easy to devote much attention to this portion of the state. This is the oldest, most settled section of northern New England; rich in traditional village greens, beautifully designed church towers, handsome old historic homes, reflecting millponds, and venerable covered bridges. Scenic beauty is present too in low wooded mountains, lakes bordered by pines and birches, and winding, rushing streams.

This is the oldest, most settled section of northern New England.

As the White Mountains drop off into low forested hills to the south, New Hampshire becomes at first very woodsy and thinly populated. Here and there is a resort lake, but the towns are comparatively small. Then, as you reach the state's lower third, well-developed villages and small cities stand fairly close to each other. Some of the towns have college campuses, some have sprawling manufacturing plants, both old and new, and others possess historic neighborhoods on which much time and money have been spent to accurately recreate the past, sometimes to the point of exceeding it in levels of maintenance and appearance.

New Hampshire also has 18 miles of seacoast, a strip that is a bit different in personality and appearance than the rest of the state. Its older working harbor communities resemble those of Maine; its shorefront estates remind one of those on the Rhode Island and Connecticut shores; and the busy beaches are typical city-edge resorts without any regional stamp. In the vicinity of the Hamptons, you'll find boardwalk amusements and rows of summer rental cottages. If you want to check out all the various coastal ingredients, Route 1A follows the ocean from Seabrook Beach, at the Massachusetts border, to downtown Portsmouth, where Maine is just across the harbor. Along this short run you'll encounter every kind of oceanfront aspect from roller coasters to state parks to grounds of pretentious estates, and every type of shore from sandy beach to rocky peninsula to fishing inlet. Old towns such as Rye and New Castle offer many reminders of colonial days for history buffs; at New Castle, there is a complete historic fort.

Portsmouth presents a mixture of photographic possibilities. In the early 1980s it enjoyed an influx of new business, and for a time was regarded as one of the fastest growing small cities in the United States. The old downtown area, steeped in the storefront atmosphere of decades past, has been overlaid with crisp new structures and much modernism. But the city always had a wealth of notable historic homes, and most of these have escaped the wrecking ball, some by being moved to new locations. Several are open to the public, with period furnishings and old-fashioned gardens. A Chamber of Commerce information center will happily provide maps and refer you to photogenic old houses.

For one of the more colorful and classical old house restorations on the Atlantic coast, visit Strawberry Banke (as it is spelled, in colonial style), on Marcy Street, Route 1, and just east of the downtown area. Here you can step back into the 1700s and find much on which to focus your camera. The structures here really look like those of the 1700s, in their simplicity of style if not in their signs of age, and many of the doorways, front steps, and curving lanes make excellent pictures.

Photographers seeking an old-world island atmosphere loaded with pictorial mood possibilities might wish to take the excursion cruise to the Isles of Shoals.

Photographers seeking an old-world island atmosphere loaded with pictorial mood possibilities might wish to take the excursion cruise to the Isles of Shoals, rocky islets in the ocean with a handful of houses and a definite ability to stir the imagination. Should you regard the setting as ideal for a Victorian fiction thriller, you might enjoy reading about an actual murder on one of these islands a century ago, in which the murderer rowed to the mainland at midnight in an effort to escape detection. The New England coast abounds in yarns of the foggy night or full moon variety, and you'll find them at local libraries in many an anthology.

If you're seeking handsome village greens, bordered by fine old inns and distinguished churches, try Jaffrey, Peterborough, or Hopkinton for starters. The latter has one of the most photographed and admired church towers in New England. All three towns are on Route 202 west of Concord. For softer, more workaday village centers, but just as interesting, try Walpole, Alstead, or Marlow, in Cheshire County, west and north of Keene. Marlow has been described as "poetic" in its composition. Here plain, simple buildings in just the right places beside a double millpond create an extremely attractive scene, espe-

MARLOW.

cially in early morning when reflections are strong or when light mists cross the water.

In the Antrim area, there are many ponds and streams, some providing interesting waterfalls or crossed by old stone bridges. At Dublin, a broad lake presents fine woods and water scenes almost any time of the year. Mount Monadnock, the gently sloping but highest mountain in southern New Hampshire, often studied by geologists because of its glacial molding, rises gradually from the southern end of Dublin Lake and is frequently painted by landscape artists. Had you visited Monadnock in the fall of 1938 you might have photographed an awesome sight — the entire forested southern slope flattened by the force of the great hurricane of that year. Only recently have the scars of that vast bowling-over finally disappeared from casual sight. Because of its gradual slope, Monadnock is easier to climb than most New Hampshire mountains.

The Connecticut River, winding Rhine-like between New Hampshire and Vermont, provides many a photographable spot. If you want to follow it for any distance, Route 5 and I-91 stay close on the Vermont side, the interstate taking the higher more scenic sweeps; Route 5 hugging the river bank and its villages.

At Hanover, on the New Hampshire side, is Dart-

mouth College, one of the original nine ivy league colleges chartered under the British Crown. It can be reached easily from I-91 or Route 5 by crossing the river at Norwich, four miles north of White River Junction (Exit 13 on I-91). Dartmouth enjoys one of the more picturesque college settings in New England, and a number of old classical buildings on the campus make fine pictorial subjects. At West Chesterfield, almost opposite Brattleboro, Vermont, there's an interesting antique carriage and sleigh museum.

Concord provides more state capital scenery to photograph. The capitol building here faces east, so a morning shot is likely best, and there are a couple of interesting statues on the capital building grounds that you might try to include for foreground interest.

For vacation-type scenic shots, don't forget the lakes. Lake Winnipesaukee sprawls for 25 irregular miles through a hilly, wooded region in the east central part of the state, not quite into the White Mountains, although the mountains are visible from its northern end. There are many opportunities for boating and watersports scenes here, from the shores or from the large excursion boats, at least one of which takes in 50 miles of lake cruising on its daily voyages.

Newfound Lake, to the west, and Squam Lake (which became "Golden Pond" in the movie of that name), to the north, are perhaps less populated by vacationers than Winnipesaukee, but have more of a north woods scenic touch to their shores.

To round out the sights in southern New Hampshire, you might find subjects of great rural interest along the lesser traveled roads east of Concord and Manchester. The area abounds with tidy little towns with rustic charm, rushing streams, and old white New England houses. Manchester, the state's largest city, although heavily commercial and industrial at its heart, boasts a restored row of huge brick mill buildings, the remains of what was once the largest textile mill in New England.

Nashua, devasted by fire in the 1930s, has regrown into a busy city, but has unfortunately lost many of its past-century architectural gems. If you're traveling with children or would like to photograph some animals, the long-popular Benson Animal Farm is at Hudson, just east of Nashua.

WAITS RIVER.

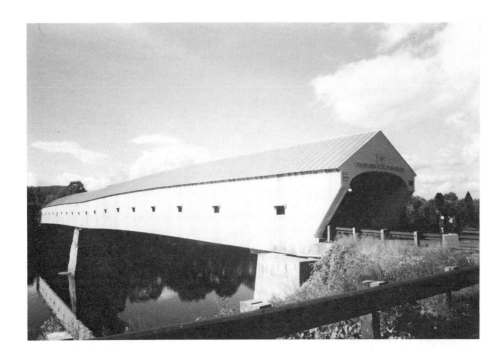

VERMONT

Vermont is basically more leafy, woodsy, and classically rustic than New Hampshire. There seem to be more working farms here, even though the state has its share of large summer homes and country estates. Its mountains are more evenly forest covered and are softer in appearance, less rocky and precipitous than those of New Hampshire. As local geologists like to say with a twinkle in their eye, the great glacier scraped the topsoil off New Hampshire's White Mountains and deposited it in Vermont.

THE LARGEST COVERED BRIDGE IN THE UNITED STATES AT WINDSOR.

The towns of Vermont have a tidy, well-kept character and a settled, at peace with the world aspect that is often immediately relaxing to the newcomer. The large, century-old churches and homesteads, so conspicuously present on village streets, were usually built with a simple but dignified style of architecture that has suited all areas. In most places, the appearance of older structures has been faithfully and proudly maintained.

The Green Mountains stretch like an almost unbroken divider down the length of Vermont, just inside the state's western edge. The only true gap through the high ridge is behind Burlington, where Routes 2

and I-89 sweep along beside the Winooski River.
Farther south, slight dips in the mountain skyline do
afford highways 4,11, and 9 reasonably level routes,
though they are not without their share of slopes and
climbs. Some roads make it across the mountains
where there doesn't seem to be any usable pass at
all. The road over Lincoln Gap, for example, between
Warren and Lincoln, negotiates what is perhaps the
steepest sustained grade of any paved road in New
England, snaking its way curve after curve up the
side of a formidable mountain — but the view at the
top is stupendous.

The Green Mountain barrier creates a sociological
division as well as a natural one. West of the mountains, along the New York state line, Vermont is a bit
more built up and commercially modern than east of
the mountains. Burlington, the state's largest city, is a
clean-cut, busy-looking town with electronics firms,
several colleges, and a prestigious medical center. Its
modern suburbs spread far along the shores of Lake
Champlain and inland toward the high mountains. It
is less typically New England than the rest of
Vermont, yet it does have a core of fine old photogenic churches and university buildings.

The Green Mountain barrier creates a sociological division as well as a natural one.

East of the Green Mountains, the state is more
rural, more heavily farmed, and more tranquil. To the
north, peaceful farms spread over the rolling hills; to
the south, picture-book villages with classic old
church towers sit quietly amid heavily wooded
mountains. Along the Connecticut River, a number of
unchanging shore towns, some of them picturesque,
some with prominent vestiges of old industry, stand
at intervals.

Vermont's climate is well balanced, with admittedly
cold and snowy winters, but summers that can get
downright hot, especially in the low-altitude
Champlain Valley and southward along the Connecticut River.

Champlain Area

THERE ARE MAGNIFICENT views of New York's
Adirondack Mountains from Burlington and the shore
hills along Lake Champlain, as well as from the ferries that cross the lake.

In Burlington itself, there's Battery Park at the foot
of Main Street, just off Route 7 in the downtown area,
where people have been photographing the view for
generations. Some of the finest sunsets have been
photographed here, sometimes enhanced by the

golden wake of a ferry in the foreground. The mountains, although famously photogenic, are nevertheless distant, and a telephoto lens is strongly advised for best results.

If you follow Route 7 southward from Burlington through Shelburne and Charlotte you will find points that offer good glimpses of the distant mountains, especially the top of 980-foot Mount Philo, just south of Charlotte. Although comparatively speaking, Mount Philo is just a high hill, it has an easy state park road winding to its summit, and there are fine unobstructed views of Lake Champlain and the Adirondacks beyond.

The ferries cross Lake Champlain from the foot of King Street in downtown Burlington and from the harbor in Charlotte, just off Route 7, 10 miles south of Burlington. The Charlotte ferry is much faster in crossing, should you wish to use it purely for scenic photography.

Vermont's own closer Green Mountains create some fine mountain vistas, even though they have fewer isolated peaks than the White Mountains or the Adirondacks and therefore present from a distance more of a solid, high green skyline. Get close into them, of course, and you'll find individual peaks of note. The Camel's Hump, Vermont's second highest mountain, is particularly photogenic; there are great views of it from Routes 2 and 100 in the Watertown area, just east of Burlington.

Mount Mansfield, the highest in Vermont, rises directly behind the Burlington city area. If you want a good record shot of it, drive along Route 15 between Essex Junction (a Burlington suburb) and Jeffersonville. But if you'd like more intimate photos of Mansfield, by all means follow Route 108 southward from Jeffersonville to Stowe. Route 108 leads up and over the high shoulders of Mount Mansfield, passes close behind its summit, and barely squeezes through narrow Smugglers Notch, a cleft strewn with enormous boulders that is one of the highest passes in New England.

Smugglers Notch is so named because Confederate sympathizers used it during the Civil War to smuggle Canadian supplies past Yankee eyes. The smugglers could not have had an easy time of it. Today's paved highway barely makes it through, twisting and turning narrowly between tumbled boulders the size of cottages. A small clearing provides parking space and although the scene may suggest the axe-work of a mad giant, it is one of wild beauty, with much to interest the photographer.

Smugglers Notch, a cleft strewn with enormous boulders, is one of the highest passes in New England.

The boulders have gradually separated from the rugged cliffs through the centuries, as ice and moisture have widened the cracks left by the continental glacier. They now lie about in a haphazard jumble, in some places atop each other with tunnel gaps beneath. The steep cliffs rise sharply behind the boulders, and you can often see and photograph alpine climbers in practice sessions, inching their way up the rock faces.

Continuing on, Route 108 slowly descends into Stowe, a summer retreat and prominent winter ski area long known for its attractive streets, buildings, and "Christmas card" setting. From Stowe to Waterbury, tiny villages adorn the ribboning road, always with a jumble of forested slopes behind them. To the southwest, Camel's Hump Mountain can be seen with its distinctive half-dome rearing at the crest of the Green Mountain chain, a good mountain subject for a telephoto lens. This is also a great area for photogenic roadside stands and antique shops.

Stowe, a summer retreat and prominent winter ski area, is long known for its attractive streets, buildings, and "Christmas card" setting.

Looking back westward a bit, the islands of Champlain Lake, traversed by Route 2 as it island hops to New York State north of Burlington, are worthy of exploration. Largely farm and meadow, with frequent attractive coves, they afford both inland and lakeshore beauty, and in clear weather, both the Green Mountains and the Adirondacks present a glorious spectacle in misty green.

Historic and Architectural Interest

ARCHITECTURE OF NOTE abounds along the western edge of Vermont. Burlington itself, in addition to the fine old buildings on the University of Vermont campus, has a number of splendid old churches and public buildings, the most photogenic of which is likely the tall Unitarian church in the heart of the downtown area. This venerable ornate tower is surrounded by lawns and trees and can be photographed well if care is taken to approach it from a good angle.

South of Burlington, Route 7 will take you through Shelburne, Charlotte, and Vergennes, in each of which you'll find old churches and other structures of photographic interest. Shelburne is the site of Shelburne Museum, whose handsome collection of buildings of the past, garnered from various corners of New England, spreads over many acres. There is much to attract the photographer here, including a

blacksmith shop, a one-room schoolhouse, a covered bridge, and a large side-wheel steamboat.

Middlebury, 15 miles south of Vergennes, on Route 7, is a classic town, with streets, common, college campus, and tall spires to attract the camera. The tall, magnificent Congregational church at the corner of the common will intrigue you, but may prove to be a difficult subject because of its closeness to the street and other buildings. Here, as with other tall towers, if backing away proves unworkable because of intervening power poles, structures, or parked vehicles, we suggest the one quick feasible solution — stand smack in front of the building and shoot straight upward for an angle view.

A word here about angle shots in general: To get an effective angle shot of any tall structure — a church steeple, a skyscraper, or whatever — get as close to the building as you can, so that the steepness effect dominates your picture without giving a "falling-over-backward" appearance. Then position your camera so that the tower is slanted toward the upper *left* corner of the picture in your viewer. Somehow, an upper *right* corner tilt usually looks awkward and wrong.

Northern Vermont

THE DOMINANT ROUTES across northern Vermont are 2, 15, and 302 east-west, and I-89 slanting northwest to southeast. All will afford top scenic vistas, although 302 is most often used for quick tours as it short-cuts to the White Mountains and passes through a region of very picturesque side roads east of Barre. I-89 will speed you to lower New Hampshire, showing you an abundance of farm and mountain views, though not as intimately as will the lesser roads.

Following Route 2 straight east to Saint Johnsbury and then veering north on Route 5 will take you into the Burke Mountain region, where farms, rolling meadows, small country villages, and a few isolated high mountains provide extremely photogenic backgrounds. Burke Mountain itself, rising heftily behind old red barns or large farmhouses, is often photographed for calendars.

We've been talking about east-west routes, but before you get very far east of the Burlington area you'll cross Route 100, a north-south road that is thoroughly worth exploration. This road, meandering down the heart of the state, is undoubtedly Vermont's most scenic and charming route. It takes you to numerous photogenic sights, both natural and otherwise, virtually all of them typically Vermont. It is well worth following in its entirety to the Massachusetts border if you have the time.

Just a few of the photogenic highlights to be encountered along Route 100 are Waitsfield, with its fine old village; Mad River, racing before a mountain backdrop; impressive Moss Glen Falls; Gifford Woods State Park; President Coolidge's home at Plymouth Union; Weston, with its much-photographed common and much-patronized old shops; and finally, the mountain heart of southern Vermont.

There is a cluster of picturesque villages here, of which Waits River is perhaps the classic example.

Don't expect a sophisticated metropolitan city if you visit Montpelier, one of the smallest state capitals in the United States. It is a neat and pleasant overgrown country village with a handsome golden-domed capitol building at its center. Set against a forested slope with a broad green lawn before it, the capitol building makes an excellent photographic subject. It can be reached without the traffic and parking problems so often encountered in larger cities.

Just a few miles east of Montpelier there's an eye-catching subject of a non scenic nature that draws many visitors annually — the marble quarries at Barre. Open to the public, they display canyon-sized quarry pits and much intriguing use of equipment.

The "Post Card Villages"

BETWEEN MONTPELIER and the Connecticut River, on Route 302, there are several side roads that present close views of those church-steepled villages that are often photographed and that typify Vermont to many Americans. We suggest Route 110 southward through Washington to Chelsea, returning to 302 by way of Corinth Corners, South Corners, and Route 25, the latter taking you through Waits River and West Topsham. There is a cluster of picturesque villages here, of which Waits River is perhaps the classic example. At Waits River, turn west at the church in the village center and go straight up the little hill for a few hundred yards. Looking back on the village from here, you'll recognize a church-centered rural village scene that you've no doubt seen more than once on calendars and in magazines. Photographed again and again, it is an attractive panorama in any season, especially autumn.

The Northern Lakes

THE VERMONT COUNTRYSIDE cannot boast the strong scatterings of lakes that grace Maine and New Hampshire, but it does have at least one true gem: Lake Willoughby.

This comparatively unsung seven-mile stretch of water lies in the northeast portion of the state about 25 miles north of Saint Johnsbury, just off Routes 5 or I-91 and directly on Route 5A. Uncluttered by large tourist towns, this small but beautiful lake is closely bordered by forested mountains, which at some points rise directly from its shores, creating magnificent scenic views that change in character with the variations of sky and weather.

Farther north, straddling the Canadian border, is the much wider and larger Lake Memphremagog. Newport, Vermont, spreads along its southern end, a busy town with touches of French Canada and reminders of an earlier frontier age. There is mountain scenery along the lake shore here too, although the higher peaks are in Quebec.

Central Vermont

IF YOU SHOULD enter Vermont from the Lake George or Ticonderoga areas of New York State, chances are you'll come in on Route 4 to Rutland and then drive across mid-Vermont toward White River Junction. However you travel, this general area has much to offer photographically. Route 4 will take you smoothly and quickly over the Green Mountains to the forest and farm region of Bridgewater, where you'll pass steep mountain slopes, picturesque rushing creeks, and many a well-placed farmhouse or old red barn.

Woodstock, between Bridgewater and White River Junction, is one of Vermont's more attractive villages, loaded with big maples and birches, fine old homes in beautifully maintained condition, a number of colorful gardens, and a trio of short, old-fashioned bridges that make town strolling a pleasure. The tree-shaded common will entice camera use, and because power lines are underground here, your photos will be free of distracting wires. Picturesque church towers? Yes, indeed; four that claim bells cast by Paul Revere.

East of Woodstock is Taftsville, with an old red covered bridge (unfortunately boxed in by heavy commercial construction), and then Queechee, with its 160-foot gorge that never ceases to surprise newcomers. It is difficult to photograph effectively, but is well worth the stop, if just to look down into the canyon from the bridge.

The Connecticut River flows lazily along the eastern edge of Vermont, and if you want to follow it through its old river towns, you can do so on Route 5 with a minimum of local traffic to impede you. No really grand scenery along here, although Mount Ascutney presents a high handsome profile as you proceed south of White River Junction. The river's Great Bend, at Newbury, — shot from a point on Route 5 where the view is downriver past a large red barn, directly toward the mountains of New Hampshire — has been a favored photo subject for calendars. The only drawback here is that it's difficult to find a fresh viewpoint. The specific spot that offers superb composition is the precise view described above that everyone has taken through the years.

The Connecticut River towns are interesting in that they have changed little for many decades.

The Connecticut River towns are interesting in that they have changed little for many decades. Old factories and commercial districts do cancel their attractiveness in some instances, but there are some fine old neighborhoods of venerable homes and any number of striking church towers. Bradford and Norwich are particularly attractive in this respect. At Windsor there are a number of historic buildings, including old Constitution House, in which Vermont was signed into being as an independent republic, 14 years before becoming the fourteenth state.

Southern Vermont

SOUTHERN VERMONT IS less basically farm rural than the northern and central areas, and its towns are a bit more touched by city hands, but its high, restfully forested mountains have led many to consider it the state's most beautiful sector. Several of the mountain villages have become focal points for urbanites who have broken away for summers of rural quietude.

Route 9 is the east-west artery across lower Vermont, linking Vermont with the Albany area of New York on the west and the southern counties of New Hampshire on the east. Bennington, close to the New York line, is a busy, growing town with large shopping malls, fine old architectural specimens, a college, and the prominent 300-foot landmark that is Bennington Battle Monument.

Brattleboro, at the eastern end of Vermont's Route

A WINTERSCAPE NEAR POWNAL.

9, is a smaller business community, a bit less modern, but much beloved by those who have had ties with it through the years. Between Bennington and Brattleboro are broken ridges of beautifully forested mountains, through which Route 9 winds, dips, and climbs, encountering very few villages, but passing widely scattered assortments of basket and cheese shops, rustic restaurants, and scenic outlooks.

Midway across the state on Route 9 is Wilmington, a small but thriving rural shopping center standing at the entrance to scenic Dover Valley, the site of Mount Snow and much winter ski activity.

Villages of the Past

FOR A WORTHWHILE side route, especially if you're interested in "character" structures of the past, we strongly suggest Route 30 northwest out of Brattleboro. The neat, attractive towns of Dummerston, West Dummerston, Newfane, and Townshend, with attractive commons and fine his-

toric structures, add some of the finer aspects of country living to the natural forest and mountain countryside.

Newfane, with its meticulously maintained historic courthouse and tall white Congregational church, presents a "pedigreed" common that is one of the most photographed in New England. You can photograph this village center from many viewpoints with a minimum of concern about foreground appearance or objects being in the way. Side-road excursions in this area will often produce striking scenic mixtures of mountain, stream, and colorful farm. This is a great region to photograph in autumn and winter, as well as in summer.

Additional handsome neighborhoods and well-kept houses of the past may be found in Manchester, a few miles north of Bennington. Here great houses line the main streets, standing far back from the curbs in beautifully maintained gardens and grounds. An uncrowded but expanding tourist center, Manchester is known for its large antique shops and art galleries, as well as for fine mountain scenery. Some of the steepest mountain slopes in Vermont can also be photographed at Manchester, where massive peaks such as 3,800-foot Equinox Mountain tower close above the village. There's an old toll road to the summit of Equinox, where there are magnificent panoramic outlooks.

THE MINUTEMAN,
CONCORD.

MASSACHUSETTS

Eastern Massachusetts

The western and eastern regions of Massachusetts are two very different kettles of fish. Western Massachusetts, that is, the part of the Commonwealth lying west of the Connecticut River, is woody, hilly, and rural. Eastern Massachusetts, though thoroughly New England and filled with reminders of history, is dominated by the sprawling Boston metropolitan area.

To explore eastern Massachusetts effectively, one must understand something of what Boston is — as a city and as an enormous area full of people and activity. If you look at the census figures for Boston, you'll find a deceptively low population. Boston's city boundaries are close to its downtown, and much of its population is counted in a dozen or more sur-

THE WHIPPLE HOUSE, 1640, IN IPSWICH, ONE OF THE OLDEST HOUSES IN THE UNITED STATES.

rounding cities and towns. Actually, although the city of Boston itself ranks only twentieth in size in the United States at this writing, the Boston metropolitan area ranks seventh among such areas, with approximately four million people — topping the metropolitan areas of Houston, Dallas, or Washington, D.C.

Boston, an old city with avenues of traffic built on a pattern of colonial lanes, is admittedly tough to drive around in, particularly for the stranger (with or without maps at hand). There are rivers, harbor indentations, bridges, tunnels, and elevated expressways, all with sudden and sharply turning exit and entrance ramps, many of which are difficult to get into if you are locked in heavy traffic or see them too late. And if you think that you've left the city once you've gone a mile or two away from downtown, you may be dismayed to note that a strictly urban landscape goes on for many miles. The Boston area is a conglomeration of long built-up towns and cities, some of them very old, many of them very congested, and all of them merging into each other so that one is indistinguishable from the other.

But don't let us scare you away. It's a great city with much to see. Just be prepared, select your route carefully in advance on a good city map, and above all avoid rush hours. This writer has made a number of relaxing photographic visits to Boston, chiefly on Sunday mornings, when reaching key downtown locations is almost ridiculously easy.

You'll find Boston by and large a friendly city with many strong and varying personality traits.

Although it has all the ills of a congested modern metropolis, you'll find Boston by and large a friendly city with many strong and varying personality traits. It is an informal city, and its people tend to be much more talkative, good humored, and unpretentious than those of, say, quieter Philadelphia or more poker-faced New York. It is a colorful city, and many places and objects here may not be the biggest of their kind, but may well have more "personality."

To limit our discussion strictly to the places in Boston and vicinity that are of prime photographic importance, lest we write an entire book about Boston, we'll begin properly with the city's downtown area.

Much like New York's lower Manhattan, downtown Boston is a narrow, harbor-bordered area with an awful lot crammed into it and a goodly number of twisting, one-way colonial streets. We would not recommend at attempt to drive to individual inner city locations — park for the duration of your downtown visit, either in a parking garage or partly out of the city at a rapid transit station. If you don't mind walking, you can see a great deal in a short time. You will need your car or other transportation to visit the universities, museums, and historical attractions across the Charles River from downtown, but more about that later.

Boston Common and the Public Garden are at the city's traditional heart; both are squared-off areas of green trees, lawns, fountains, and playgrounds, surrounded by tall buildings and ornate edifices. An hour's wandering about here can bring you a wealth of Boston "pictureture"; everything from shots of the state capitol and various historic structures to close-ups of tourist boats gliding under pond footbridges and children playing at the bases of tall statues.

The double park offers views of office buildings through and above stately old trees; there are the beautiful architectural church towers, saturated with storied history, and you'll find blossoming trees and shrubs in spring, golden foliage in fall.

Perhaps the chief photographic challenge here, if you like challenges, is the great golden-domed Massachusetts State House, one of the toughest capitol buildings to photograph correctly. It is perched on sharply rising ground, and you have to look up at it as you stand on Beacon Street in front of it. Because it is hemmed in by tall trees and bordered by other buildings, you can't get a decent shot of it by walking up or down the street; if you move back and downward into the common, heavy foliage tends to block your view. Moreover, you'll find yourself pointing your camera upward, giving the building that "falling over backward" effect. But if you check various angles and use a wide-angle lens, you'll eventually find spots from which you can gain an acceptable shot. I know that some photographers give up the search, as I've seen the building "leaning backward" in pictorial books whose editors should normally frown on such photographic ineptitude.

Beacon Hill rises immediately north of Boston Common, behind Beacon Street, and here local professional people continue to own or rent lodgings in one of the most intriguing and distinctive neighborhoods in any American city. If streets of old town houses or the architectural details of eras long past interest you, you can have a field day here. Facades, ornate entrances, stone steps, ivied walls, and old iron gates, all dripping with suggestions of a distant past, have long provided the basis for much creative photography here.

Commonwealth Avenue heads westward from the public garden and can provide you with good gener-

Beacon Hill. . . one of the most intriguing and distinctive neighborhoods in any American city.

al shots of a mansion-lined thoroughfare. The boulevard islands in the center are wide and filled with trees and shrubs, which are particularly photogenic when spring blossoms prevail.

Eastward from the common, the streets become narrow and elbowing. Tall financial towers rise at every bend, with a number of small shops and restaurants existing in the crevices between them, in some instances occupying short structures of "quaint" architecture from the past. There is flavor enough here to remind you that you are still in New England, not Chicago or New York. Close by are such notable landmarks as Faneuil Hall, the Old State House, and the venerable Old South Meeting House, built in 1729, but looking more as though it were a product of the present century. Although it may not look its age, Old South Meeting House is a handsome church to photograph. Choose the right vantage point and you'll find you can photograph the tower in silhouette against some of Boston's taller office buildings, creating an interesting contrast.

There is flavor enough here to remind you that you are still in New England, not Chicago or New York.

The old Haymarket stalls once offered a busy, colorful outdoor area of produce marketing virtually in the shadow of Faneuil Hall. All this has now been moved into the new Quincy Market, an adjoining modernized area that includes gourmet shops and restaurants — an extremely popular spot. You can still catch some of the color and personality of the original Haymarket on Saturday mornings, when vendors present a modified outdoor version of the original just outside Quincy Market. Many of the warehouses and other older structures in the vicinity of Quincy Market have recently been leveled, and a vast red brick campus encompasses City Hall and other civic structures, providing much of interest for photographers. Farther to the north and east, beyond the elevated Fitzgerald Expressway, Boston's oldest neighborhood spreads along the waterfront, and here you can find such notable historical gems as Paul Revere's house and the Old North Church.

For panoramic views of the city, go back the other way a half-mile or so to Copley Square with its architecturally honored Trinity Church and Boston Public Library, and the sheer 60-story rise of the John Hancock Tower. The Hancock's glass walls clearly mirror the nearby structures and will at times reflect the sun so strongly that objects in the park area below cast double shadows. If you're a science fiction fan, you'll be reminded of those stories of planets with two suns.

Visit the observation deck atop the Hancock Tower

and you'll have a magnificent view of the city and its rivers and harbor spreads. This is a good place to orient yourself as to where things are in the area. On a clear day you can see the White Mountains from here, as tiny blurs on the northern horizon. Here, as on other observation decks of this kind, be aware of what you are aiming your camera through. Window panes tinted to reduce glare can throw off your exposures and color renditions.

A few blocks farther south, the Prudential Center offers more tall buildings, including the 52-story "Pru" with another popular observation deck. There are elevated promenades here and many outdoor spots from which to take a wide variety of urban shots.

Copley Place, a block east of Copley Square, is one of those charismatic indoor shopping malls where multilevels, indoor fountains, and gleaming escalators provide a "twenty-first-century" aura, and there is enough light for good shots with ASA 400 film.

Cross the Charles River and you're in Cambridge or Charlestown, each a separate city, but completely an extension of Boston in appearance and character. In Charlestown stands the famous old Bunker Hill Monument, surrounded by a small park with nineteenth-century period houses along its bordering streets. Down the hill from the monument the *U.S.S. Constitution*, "Old Ironsides," floats at its pier in dark-wooded dignity. Built in 1797, it is the oldest commissioned vessel afloat in the United States. (Her almost-sister, the *Constellation*, berthed in Baltimore, is a few days older but holds no commission or lingering official association with the United States Navy.) You may photograph Old Ironsides from all angles and indoors with available light if you've got fast film.

In Cambridge, the great array of classical buildings in and around the campuses of Harvard University and the Massachusetts Institute of Technology provide an awesome implication of accumulated knowledge, as well as fine photographic subjects. A walk along the edge of the Charles River may inspire you to use up a fair amount of film; there are excellent views of the Boston skyline and of interesting boating of all kinds, including rowing, if you're there at the right time.

As in most waterfront cities, there are excursion boats to take you out under the bridges and across the harbor — a good sail that can reward you photographically with fine shots of skyline, ocean steamships, and even Minot Lighthouse, if your craft ventures out that far.

In Charlestown stands the famous old Bunker Hill Monument, surrounded by a small park with nineteenth-century period houses along its bordering streets.

Northward away from Boston, chiefly along Route 1A, are many famous old towns that are loaded with buildings and monuments of historical significance. For a rocky shore in a quiet scene, drive out to Nahant on the causeway from Lynn, on Route 1A, 10 miles north of Boston. Nahant is a community of old, typically New England shore houses of the larger sort, set at the end of a narrow rocky peninsula. At beach access points here you can photograph waves

THE PRUDENTIAL TOWER. THE COMICAL FACE WAS PART OF THE DECOR FOR A LOCAL EVENT.

swirling between rocky parapets, and some of the weather-beaten old houses make good subjects as well.

North of Lynn, there are a number of seaside communities with historic landmarks, interesting old New England structures, and picturesque, twisting lanes. Salem, on Route 1A, five miles north of Lynn, is rich in solid old houses that thoroughly look their part. Many houses here are famous for both their appearance and their history, including Pinckney House with its gothic detail; the Corwin or "Witch House," associated with the days of witchcraft trials; the house Hawthorne used as a model for *The House of Seven Gables*; and others. These houses have a history-laden aura about them that transfers easily to film, and they are easy to photograph from the quiet streets.

At Ipswich, on Route 1A 12 miles north of Salem, there's a dark old house with a well-kept garden that is considered the oldest wooden house in the United States. This is the Whipple House, built in the late 1630s. Strongly Elizabethan in character, it makes an excellent photographic appearance, particularly from the side of the fenced garden.

Marblehead, east of Salem on Route 114, in addition to the usual notable edifices, possesses one of the most beautiful yachting harbors on the Atlantic coast. Drive up on the heights above the water on a sunny day when scores of sailing craft dot the harbor, and you'll have as pretty a boating view as you could hope for. The last week of July is Race Week, a prime time occasion for anyone who loves to photograph modern sailing craft.

Marblehead possesses one of the most beautiful yachting harbors on the Atlantic coast.

The Cape Ann peninsula, at the eastern end of Route 128 which 1A intersects north of Salem, holds a wealth of worthy subject matter along its rocky shores. Routes 127 and 127A will, between them, take you on a complete swing around the Cape. At Gloucester Harbor, on Route 127, there are commercial fishing craft of all sizes and kinds, and on Gloucester's avenued bayfront is the much-photographed statue of the ancient mariner-fisherman firmly gripping his wheel. You can easily photograph him, either from a slight distance with the surrounding scene in the background, or up close with all the details clear and the open sky as a backdrop.

Many shutters are snapped at Rockport, in another part of Cape Ann, a busy collection of colorful shops and art galleries strung out along a harbor edge. If you're not photographing the shopping scene you can point your camera between structures and catch

THE OLD MARINER STATUE
FACING GLOUCESTER HARBOR.

interesting small boats at their moorings. The famous "Motif Number One" is here — a water's edge shed used for years as a recommended basic for practicing artists.

South of Boston, through Quincy, the urban scene extends virtually all the way to Plymouth with its famous canopied Plymouth Rock and berthed replica of the *Mayflower*. There are many interesting scenes and houses here too, including a detailed re-creation of the Plymouth colony of the 1620s, complete with costumed "inhabitants" who go about in mimic of the original colonists.

There is more visible history on Route 2A west of Boston, much of it inviting to photograph, including the two Minuteman statues, one at the famous Old North Bridge in Concord, the other at the Lexington Battle Green; Walden Pond and a number of historic houses, which include The Old Manse on Monument Road in Concord, lived in at different times by both Hawthorne and Emerson; Orchard House on Lexington Road in Concord, where Louisa May Alcott once lived; The Wayside on Lexington Road in Concord, where Miss Alcott spent a portion of her childhood; and Emerson House at 28 Cambridge Turnpike. We gave additional detail to this area in the spring chapter because of the great activity always scheduled for Patriot's Day, but of course both the colonial beauty and the historical significance of Concord and Lexington are worth seeing and photographing at any time of the year.

Along the top of eastern Massachusetts, much urban renewal has removed many of the monstrous brick factories that once stood as the huge landmarks of an era, but a few do remain, particularly in Lowell, where national and state historical parks include restored factory sections and other re-creations of an industrial past.

Worcester, where I-290 and I-190 meet, isn't often mentioned as a traveler's destination, but it is, after all the third largest city in New England. For a city whose basic industry is manufacturing, it has a fine array of parks, college campuses, monuments, and classic old buildings, as well as beautiful suburban lakes, long loved by canoeists. The trouble is, if the traveler comes to Worcester after having visited much of greater Boston's wealth of architectural and historical sites, it is easy to regard Worcester as an anticlimactic. But a good way to introduce yourself to Worcester and to see whether or not it whets your photographic appetite is to drive through it on I-290. This elevated highway whisks you right into the heart of the city, past downtown office buildings, a number of prominent landmarks, and almost along the grandstand edge at Holy Cross Stadium. If you want a good shot of the downtown area, take it through the car window (while someone else is driving). You just don't see the city well from anywhere else.

If you like photographing old shops and houses of the past that have been gathered together in re-created communities, visit Sturbridge Village, 17 miles southwest of Worcester along Route 20 or via the Massachusetts Turnpike. There is enough nostalgic New England here to hold your attention for a couple of full days — everything from carriages and early craft equipment to a complete village green.

Cape Cod and the Islands

CAPE COD IS JUST what it has always been, and what you anticipate it to be — pure New England in a seaside version. It is reached most directly from Boston via Route 3, which joins and becomes Route 6 when it reaches the Cape, and from points west via I-195 and I-495, which merge and become what is first known as Route 25, and soon after as Route 28. (The changes are well posted on the highways; nothing is likely to confuse.)

Cape Cod is just what it has always been, and what you anticipate it to be — pure New England in a seaside version.

Route 6A, paralleling Route 6 on the Cape's bay side, is a comparatively slow road, but a gem for local sightseeing. On this route you'll encounter, for example, one of the Cape's most attractive towns almost immediately. Sandwich is one of those communities steeped in sturdy New England charm, where roads curve into town across and beside attractive inlets, providing many vantage points for photographing traditional house and church tower settings as viewed across the water.

Other such towns are Chatham, at the easternmost point on Route 28, and Wellfleet, on Route 6 near the tip of the Cape. The harbors of these communities are rich in that special type of old-fashioned maritime atmosphere so loved by artists and creative photographers. You will likely find your own favorites among the similar towns located along Routes 6, 6A, and 28 and, as you may well discover, one of the problems associated with exploring Cape Cod is that you will likely use up entirely too much film!

For excellent opportunities in creative nature photography, don't overlook the Cape Cod National Seashore, which follows the ocean edge along virtually all of the Cape's slender, northward-curving hook, from Nauset Beach to Provincetown. Route 6 advanced close behind it, providing easy access at various points.

At Nauset Beach you'll find every aspect of the surf-swept, dune-crested beach so admired by those devoted to natural settings, plus a few more. There are long curling breakers that you can photograph with grass-topped dunes in the foreground, often with the look of an enchanting, undiscovered shore.

You can find such intriguing natural subjects as beach plums, dwarf pines, and berry clusters, and even an occasional bit of interesting driftwood or perhaps the lingering remains of an old shipwreck.

Nature trails abound in the National Seashore, if you like to hike with your camera. Most of these are in the seashore's wider region, between Wellfleet and Truro, their access points indicated on turn-offs from Route 6. Wildlife opportunities, high dunes, wide mysterious pools, and lonely stretches of marsh and meadow suggestive of storied English or Scottish moors, are all here for your eyes and camera. The patient, observant hiker can spot a wide variety of birds, wildfowl, and unusual plants.

The outer hook of the Cape, with the National Seashore and the old towns of Eastham, Truro, and Provincetown, is the distilled essence of everything that suggests or pertains to Cape Cod. There are high bluffs and grass-topped dunes; little resort communities with inviting inns and restaurants; artist colonies; and relics of shipwreck and Coast Guard history.

Provincetown remains a photogenic gem despite its ever-expanding list of eateries and "quaint" or "cute" gift shops.

Provincetown remains a photogenic gem despite its ever-expanding list of eateries and "quaint" or "cute" gift shops. It's a great place to move about with your camera, checking scenes from varying angles and seeking out small subjects such as artistic signs and odd gateposts and a fairly colorful Bohemian human interest atmosphere. The creative photographer or artist may prefer to visit Province-town, or all of Cape Cod, for that matter, in fall or spring, as tourist traffic has admittedly become almost a bit too much in summer.

Travelers to Cape Cod are often lured seaward by New England's most populated and visited islands: Martha's Vineyard and Nantucket. Martha's Vineyard, the larger of the two, has scenic boating harbors, fine beaches, a number of small, picturesque, "unspoiled" shore communities, and stretches of coastline bordered by low cliffs.

Nantucket, farther out to sea, has been much less built upon than Martha's Vineyard, and what has been built clings religiously to the styles and appearances of the island's seagoing past. Here are fine old streets lined with sea captains' homes, and a "salty" harbor that retains many memories of the whaling days of the early nineteenth century. Beyond the town, Nantucket is a delightful wilderness of wildflowers and berries, bordered by tumbling surf and broken here and there by small clusters of summer homes. Nantucket can be reached by year-found ferry from Hyannis (Route 28 on Cape Cod), and by summer ferry from Woods Hole, off Route 28 at Falmouth to Woods Hole Road.

On the Massachusetts mainland west of the islands, the old port of New Bedford also lures maritime buffs with lingering echoes of the days of sail and whaling at its harbor and in its museums.

Inland west of New Bedford, you'll find Fall River, which because of its location on Narragansett Bay and its proximity to Providence, is more closely related in many ways to Rhode Island than to Massachusetts. New Bedford and Fall River are both on I-195; New Bedford where Route 140 intersects and Fall River at the junction of Route 24.

If much of Fall River seems of an earlier period, it must be remembered that this is a city that prospered early in its career and then ceased to grow. One of the 20 largest cities in the United States during the glory days of the New England textile industry, Fall River doesn't make the top 100 today — a blessing in disguise, many big city residents may say.

Because much of the old was not swept away of necessity to make room for the new, you can find many turn-of-the-century homes and buildings in active use, even in downtown business blocks. Fall River citizens will of course be happy to point out that much in the way of new construction has recently taken place, particularly at the rejuvenated waterfront, where you'll find boutiques and seafood restaurants clustered near the moored battleship *U.S.S. Massachusetts*. If you happen to be a Lizzie Borden buff, you'll know where to find and photograph the famous house, which at this writing is still there (occupied by people who no doubt hope the world will someday forget).

Western Massachusetts

WESTERN MASSACHUSETTS IS dominated by the Berkshires. They are the mountains of Vermont diminishing steadily in height as you move southward, becoming the Litchfield Hills upon reaching Connecticut. They are softer of contour and more penetrable by roads. Estates, parks, and old vacation hotels help to give the region a prosperous, well-ordered, gentleman-farmer look, along with shops and organizations catering to antiques and the arts. The annual Tanglewood Music Festival is held here, and a number of prominent writers, artists, and musicians have chosen to retire or summer here — all of

which in some way tends to lead motels and restaurants to charge more than their counterparts in other areas.

THE FIRST CONGREGATIONAL CHURCH IN WILLIAMSTOWN.

But for the photographer who loves architecture, formal old village scenes, and tidy rural landscapes where stone fences or barnyard gates seem ready-prepared for picture backgrounds, this region is a delight. Churches, houses, and large inns of the past have been restored and preserved with care and fidelity, and old village streets effectively blend the unpretentious and the dignified.

Williamstown, on Route 7 near the Vermont state line, is a classic because of the Williams College campus, long regarded as one of the more noble campuses in New England. Its broad lawns and scholarly old buildings beckon to the camera as though they were assembled to do so. Another of New England's top photogenic churches, again as so often, Congregational, stands at the western end of the campus, tall and white and surrounded by well-kept lawns. Its finely built tower, with a large clock, invites a look-up angle shot, but there's enough open land on hand for your to photograph the church in its entirety from a number of directions, with or without a wide-angle lens. Catch it in winter if you can; it makes a great picture when the roof and grounds are dazzling in snow,

North and south from Williamstown along Route 7, there are many fine views of low mountains rising peacefully beyond broad meadows. If you cut back into the hills on Route 8 you'll find more and closer views of mountain heights, including an especially fine shot of Mount Greylock, Massachusetts' highest summit, at a creek crossing between Adams and Cheshire.

Route 2, running east-west across Massachusetts, provides much mountain scenery, crossing the upper Berkshires at a point where they are almost as high as the Green Mountains of Vermont. The stretch of Route 2 between North Adams and the Connecticut River has long been known as the Mohawk Trail, a name that became famous to early auto tourists in the 1920s, before highways were numbered. Many a family in those years sent postcards to friends showing the Hairpin Turn, which was then the apex of high altitude driving achievement in New England. Though less publicized today, the Hairpin Turn is still

THE SHELDON-HAWKES HOUSE IN DEERFIELD.

there, and there's ample parking space for pausing to photograph the great view westward over lower mountains into New York State. Gift shops and eating places are present for your resting pleasure too, if you like.

Eastward from the Hairpin Turn, Route 2 meanders across high forested hills, gradually descending to the Connecticut Valley. There are some very scenic spots where it crosses or borders on the lively Deerfield River, especially at Charlemont, where you'll find a conspicuous Indian statue and the excellent Bissel Bridge. At Shelburne there's a simple but unusual Flower Bridge, a rustic footbridge heavily bedecked with flowering plants, the maintained creation of a local garden club.

The lower Berkshires, as you approach Connecticut, are more heavily settled, less resemble mountains, and have a forest cover that is more broken by farms. Route 23, which winds its way east-west through the hills, is a lot slower to follow than the Massachusetts Turnpike when you're going all the way to Springfield, but it rewards patience with much rustic beauty.

The Lenox-Stockbridge area is the heart of the Berkshires in spirit as well as geographically.

The Lenox-Stockbridge area is the heart of the Berkshires in spirit as well as geographically. Here there are fine old churches, mansions, summer estates, storied old inns, quality shops with low rustic profile, art and antique galleries, and such cultural features as the Norman Rockwell Museum, the Berkshire Playhouse, and the annual Tanglewood Music Festival. The Red Lion inn on the main street of Stockbridge is the archetypical old New England summer hotel, and the big white Church-on-the-Hill makes a strong picture on a bend of Route 7 at Lenox.

Pittsfield is a growing commercial city, but Great Barrington, its smaller edition to the south, both are on Route 7, still has many fine old residential streets, monuments, and parklike intersections. Even the heart of its business district retains a personality of its own, rich in old red brick buildings and handsome storefronts. On side roads close to Great Barrington you'll find large farmhouses and barns straight out of the stuff from which greeting cards featuring the New England scene are made. South Egremont, with its heavily foliaged streets, is another such place, nice in autumn for residential foliage shots. The village claims to have the tallest balsam poplar in the United States.

Sheffield, close to the Connecticut border, once boasted of its covered bridge, still mentioned on many maps. Pending restoration, however, it is currently closed and in poor condition. The side roads branching out from Sheffield will nevertheless lead you to excellent natural scenery. A jumble of very high hills to the west provides a mountainous aspect, and Bish Bash Falls State Park is worth a visit.

Along the Connecticut River, followed pretty closely by I-91 and Route 5, there is a diversity of photographic subject matter, ranging from steeply wooded hills to city riverfronts and peaceful farmland. Springfield, close to the Connecticut line, is an old city with much that is unattractive and heavily commercial, but it does have its highlights. In the heart of the downtown area, an interesting Italianate tower looks down on a tight little enclave that has come to be known as Museum Quadrangle. Here four museums face each other as though assembled for their portraits.

The old Springfield Armory and other vintage public buildings may provide photographic subject material as well. Large and verdant Prospect Park, at the city's southern edge, contains a zoo and an attractive paddleboat lake.

In it suburbs, Springfield offers much in the way of attractive homes and grounds, especially between the city and the Connecticut line. Longmeadow, on Route 5 just south of the city limits, is particularly attractive, offering carefully maintained old houses, set far back from the road, with great old trees before them.

Northward from Springfield, the Connecticut River flows through a region that gained fame as beautifully scenic a century ago. Mount Tom, at Exit 18 on I-91, the heights of Holyoke, on Route 202 at Exit 16 on I-91, the churning Chicopee River with its mills, and picturesque South Hadley Falls, on Route 202 just east of Holyoke, are all still there today, although urban spread has admittedly dimmed much of the area for scenic photography. The region is truly conscious of its past, maintaining it where it can, but its nostalgic heritage shines chiefly today in excellent museums more than on the open land. In South Hadley, you can photograph authentic fossil dinosaur tracks at Dinosaur Land.

North of Holyoke, Northampton presents its share of venerable architecture with past-century character, including Smith College and the Massachusetts home of Calvin Coolidge. Take I-91 if you want to speed smoothly to points northward, but risk the local traffic on Route 5 if you want to see some of the many real bits and pieces of the past and those occasional photogenic river views. In the vicinity of Hatfield, you'll still see some of the lingering tobacco fields

that once spread over large portions of the Connecticut Valley.

A COLONIAL RESIDENCE
IN DEERFIELD.

East of Northhampton, on Route 9, Amherst offers two attractive college campuses: one the very old, ivied epitome of scholarly New England, the other a modernistic complex of sweeping lawns and gleaming buildings. The first is Amherst College; the second, the University of Massachusetts.

As you pass the Deerfield area, just south of Greenfield, do visit the community of historic Deerfield if you enjoy photographing the quiet elegance of the very distant past. Few historic neighborhoods anywhere make as much of an impression on lovers of old houses as does Deerfield. Here the beautifully cared-for homes go back to British colonial days, and the historic markers relate to such events as Indian attacks. Doorways, gateposts, chimneys, and other architectural features preserved from the past make great photo subjects here, as do the beautiful homes themselves. A number of the houses are open to the public under the auspices of the Deerfield Historical Society.

Just north of Greenfield, Route 2 cross the Connecticut River on a high steel bridge that offers a fine vantage point for the grand views of the river and hills. The Connecticut River resembles the Hudson here, as it veers in gradual curves between steeply sloped mountains thick with forest.

A VIEW OF MOUNT GREYLOCK
FROM ROUTE 8 IN ADAMS.

If you roam the back roads of western Massachusetts, you'll find a number of twists and turns that
will surprise and reward you with bits and pieces of
rural, small town America. At Worthington, on Route
112, for instance, a fine old clock-towered church
with a tidy village at tis back; at Goshen, Swift River,
and East Windsor, quiet village scenes; and at a number of places along Routes 116 and 143, rural areas
that have barely been touched by recent decades.

RHODE ISLAND

Northern New England, with its wealth of mountains, lakes, and scenic countryside, receives much more attention in vacation literature than does southern New England, but Rhode Island and Connecticut in New England's southern region, do contain much to see and photograph. Rhode Island, marine focused at its southern end, and largely industrial and urban at its northern end, squeeze a million people into what is the smallest land area of any state in the union.

The state's original name, as colonially chartered, was Rhode Island and Providence Plantations, a title that encompassed both the island on which the town of Newport was located and the town of Providence with its surrounding farms. Newport County today makes up the large island in Narragansett Bay, still know as Rhode. Although Providence and the mainland region today dominate the state in population, it has proved easy to shorten the state's long name to just Rhode Island.

SOME OF NEWPORT'S YACHTS.

Northern Rhode Island

ALTHOUGH THE PROVIDENCE skyline in no way challenges Boston's or Hartford's, there are tall buildings at the city's hub, which is in walking distance of the large state capitol building and the ivy league campus of Brown University. There is plenty of open park area here for good shots of the capitol and downtown buildings. Three interstates, I-95, I-195, and I-295, along with several major state routes, merge at Providence. The best way to reach the downtown area is by taking I-95 to exits 21 or 22, which place you at the center of the city. The heart of the city can be photographed well from Kennedy Plaza. Here there is room for various shots of towers both old and new, ornate and plain, along with a few monuments and other subjects of close-up interest.

Elsewhere in Providence there are other parks and public buildings of photographic interest, particularly the Roger Williams Memorial at Prospect Terrace, where a monument faces an excellent view of the city. There are also Roger Williams Park with its museum, zoo, and eighteenth-century cottage; the elegant John Brown mansion on Power Street; and The Arcade, America's first indoor shopping mall (1828), on Westminster Street. (Yes, you can still spend money in it.)

THE MARIA PITMAN HOUSE IN NEWPORT.

From Providence northward, Rhode Island is urban and industrial. Cities like Woonsocket and Pawtucket carry greater Providence's sprawl of industry up to and across the Massachusetts line. There are some nice residential areas here as well as centers of hard work, but little, really, to lure the vacationing photographer.

Narragansett Bay

IF GREAT HOUSES with a 1920s look to them and lawns that sweep down to old weathered boathouses intrigue you, there's much of that to be photographed along the western shore of Narragansett Bay in the Wickford area and elsewhere, particularly if you can get out on the water. From out on the bay, these properties present picture after picture of a bygone era of lawn parties, small boating, and the general vacationing life of the successful people of decades past. When the overnight boats ran from New York to Providence and Fall River they would occasionally turn spotlights on some of these old houses as they steamed by.

From out on the bay, these properties present picture after picture of a bygone era of lawn parties, small boating, and the general vacationing life of the successful people of decades past.

The ports of Bristol, on Route 114, and Newport contain a good share of the photogenic plums in this small state. At Newport, which, because of its size and importance in the early 1800s, very nearly became one of the east coast's major cities (it lacked only adequate bridge contact with the mainland), there is a double-barreled nostalgic attraction. Downtown, at the southern end of Route 114, is a full-fledged historical town center with gems of architectural antiquity, and out along the ocean edge, an array of turn-of-the-century mansions lines the clifftops with awesome ostentation.

Downtown Newport, where Route 114 ends, along with the much shorter local Route 214 and 138A, is the core of a very busy town in colonial days, sufficiently loaded with beautifully restored and maintained vintage structures to resemble a huge stage set. Washington Square is surrounded by notable landmarks, including 1739 Colony House, where George Washington conferred with Count Rochambeau of France on Revolutionary War strategy; the Wanton-Lyman-Hazard House, which dates to the late 1600s, and Touro Synagogue, the oldest Jewish house of worship in the United States.

Queen Anne Square, a block or two south of Washington Square, is dominated by the tower of Trinity Church, built in 1729. In each of the squares and on the streets between them, there are points from which you can capture scenes authentically colonial in appearance. Trinity Church was already more than 50 years old when George Washington attended services there, and a number of the older homes in the neighborhood have been virtually unchanged since the 1700s.

For a sudden change of pace, walk a block to the harbor's edge, where you'll not only find a busy modern harbor, but an array of boutiques and restaurants built into the remains of two venerable wharves. Because the city is congested in this area, and signs guiding the visitor to parking spaces or to specific points of interest are woefully lacking, we strongly suggest that you visit the Tourist Information Center upon arrival (this *is* flagged). The staff

AN OLD FASHIONED PRINTING SHOP IN NEWPORT.

here provide you boutifully with whatever maps, brochures, and information you need.

If you leave the downtown area by following the curve of the harbor southward, you'll find yourself almost immediately in a much more open region, with long park lawns between the road and the water, and with places to park. A monument here marks the arrival of Lafayette's forces from France during the Revolutionary War. Continue to follow the harborside road, and you'll eventually reach Brenton Point State Park, where you can look out over Narragansett Bay on one side and the Atlantic Ocean on the other.

In the late 1800s, Newport became a status symbol of grand proportions. Wealthy New York socialites strove to outdo each other in building mammoth, grandly designed oceanfront summer homes. A number of these still line the lawn-covered clifftops a mile or so southeast of the city's heart. Up close, they are ostentatiously awesome; some of the gates alone rival those of European baronial palaces. A two-and-a-half-mile clifftop path, meandering from Memorial

OFF WASHINGTON SQUARE IN NEWPORT.

Boulevard to Lands End, now provides easy photographic access to the scenic clifftop ocean views, and to what is perhaps the most impressive lineup of elegant past-era mansions.

Some of the key houses are open to the public, including The Breakers, which, like the New York and North Carolina Vanderbilt mansions, presents something of an epitome of grand furnishings and ornate interior design. It was built in the 1890s by Cornelius Vanderbilt II. The oceanfront faces east here, so that many of these big houses more or less need to be photographed in the morning or at noon if you want to have the sun on their fronts. Balcourt Castle, at the end of the long path, faces south. Streets pass fairly close to all of the mansions, so you don't have to hike the entire length of the path to see

THE STATUE OF ROCHAMBEAU
IN NEWPORT.

them all. Views along the edge of the escarpment and out to sea are also worthy of photographs.

There's still more to see and photograph in Newport, a city almost surrounded by bays, coves, harbors, and the Atlantic Ocean itself. Fort Adams State Park presents interesting harbor views, and not

THE LINDEN HOUSE, BRISTOL.

WATCH HILL.   far from the harbor you'll find both the Tennis Hall of
Fame and the Museum of Yachting. You can reach
Fort Adams State Park, only one mile from downtown, by following Wellington Avenue along the harbor edge from the downtown area. When you reach
Harrison Avenue, you'll see the state park entrance
signs. At Middletown, immediately north of downtown Newport, on either Route 114 or Route 138,
there's a photogenic working windmill at your service. This community is so close to Newport that you
may think you're still in the latter when you reach it,
but it has its own tourist information center to guide
you.

One of the most handsome suspension bridges in
the country will take you westward from Newport to
Conanicut Island, where another, smaller bridge will
advance you to the mainland. Fifteen miles northeast
of Newport you can cross another bridge to mainland
Bristol, another venerable town with echoes of the
past. There are working boatyards in Bristol, and a
colorful harbor. Nathaniel and L. Francis Herreshoff,
honored names in classic sailing craft design for
many decades, lived and worked here, and the little
seaport is still a popular boating center. At the
Herreshoff Boatyard and Marine Museum you can get
close-up shots of such things as classic bows and
bowsprit designs.

Southwestern Rhode Island

IN THE SOUTHWESTERN part of the state, traversed by Route 1, Point Judith presents an interesting seascape and lighthouse, at the end of Route 108, off Route 1. From here westward to Watch Hill, along Route 1, there is a succession of small old villages and fine beaches. Offshore, Block Island, reached by ferry from the Galilee State Pier at Point Judith, presents much the same type of hilly seaside landscape as Martha's Vineyard, but it is a shade less developed and noticeably quieter in summer activity. There are some great high cliffs here, dipping into the Atlantic Ocean, and an interesting old-fashioned harborfront where the ferry docks.

The only portion of Rhode Island to offer much in the way of woods and rolling farm country resembling the rural districts of the rest of New England is the northwest corner and downward along the Connecticut state line. Here highways wind briefly through woodlands, past beckoning ponds and old mills and alongside farms with red barns, herds of cows, and rushing streams. The chief roads for viewing this scenery are Route 44 west from Providence; the north-south Route 102, particularly in the Chepachet area, and Route 96 and 100, which wind northwest from Chepachet to Massachusetts.

OLD LIGHTHOUSE
MUSEUM, STONINGTON.

CONNECTICUT

Connecticut has room for a bit more countryside than Rhode Island, and offers the Litchfield Hills (basically, the area between Routes 7 and 8 in the northwest corner of the state), which are an extension of the Berkshires in appearance and personality, plus a varied Connecticut valley region. Long Island Sound provides the state's access to the sea, and at some of the older ports there are colorful vestiges of the busy nautical activities of a century and more ago.

THE BUTTOLPH-WILLIAMS HOUSE IN WETHERSFIELD.

The Coast

NEW LONDON, ON I-95 near the state's southeast corner, retains a busy harbor and an older section of the downtown where buildings associated with early nineteenth-century shipping remain. The Coast Guard Academy, just up the Thames River from the city, provides a handsome water's edge campus of buildings and monuments immersed in traditions of maritime life. At another institution, Connecticut College, there is an arboretum with many magnificent old trees.

At Mystic, 10 miles east of New London, on either I-95 or Route 1, is one of the major commercial restoration attractions in the east — Mystic Seaport. Here is a re-created port of whaling days, complete with many actual relics and structures of the past, and with a number of photogenic old historic vessels moored and open to the public. Most visited is likely the *Charles W. Morgan*, one of the more successful and publicized whaling vessels of the early 1800s. With her bowsprit pointing far out over the walkway at the harbors edge, she's just begging to be photographed. I missed a good shot here many years ago when my young son climbed out to the end of that bowsprit, much to the mixed amusement and consternation of sightseers and seaport personnel. Yes, he climbed back to safety, but in the excitement I failed to use my camera. We can heartily recommend all of Mystic Seaport to photographers, and you won't need a child's acrobatic stunt to get good shots.

At Old Lyme, on I-95 and 1 at the mouth of the Connecticut River, there is no longer much of an active shipping harbor, but great homes of sea captains and prosperous shippers of the past are on hand, ranging along shady streets that have not lost their long-standing charm and dignity. Another of New England's more photogenic spires, the often photographed Congregational church, faces a town square with its tall Christopher Wren steeple.

New Haven, where I-91 and I-95 meet, although still a seaport, is of course better known today for its older neighborhoods, farther back from the shore and thick with architectural classics, and for Yale University, perhaps the epitome of the grand old university in its general appearance. Enjoying a more spacious and less citified campus than Harvard, Yale abounds with buildings and greens and vantage points for interesting photographs. New Haven's central green, much like a quieter edition of the Boston Common, is also a focal point for distinguished and historic architecture in open, nicely landscaped, easy-to-photograph settings.

Several old towns on the shore of Long Island Sound boast famous old mansions and public squares. Although they are not as numerous as those in some of the more well-known historical cities, and are somewhat surrounded by modern neighborhoods, they are excellent specimens and worthy of a visit should you find yourself in town with your cam-

Here is a re-created port of whaling days, complete with many actual relics and structures of the past, and with a number of photogenic old historic vessels moored and open to the public.

era. We suggest Guilford, at Exit 58 on I-95, with its seventeenth-century Hyland House; Waterford, on Route 156 west of New London, with Harkness State Park; Groton, on I-95 just east of New London, with its 135-foot view-affording monument and the submarine *Nautilus*; and Stonington, on alternate Route 1 just east of Mystic, with its old lighthouse museum.

Stamford and Bridgeport, close to the New York City metropolitan area, are busy commercial cities, each with a number of new buildings and modern business complexes, but little to point out specifically as camera targets. The recently expanded Barnum Museum and the largest zoo in Connecticut are likely Bridgeport's chief attractions for the casual visitor passing through.

The Hartford Area

AT THE HEART OF the Connecticut, where I-91 and I-84 cross, sits Hartford, one of those cities that looks much bigger than it is. Although it is not even the largest city in Connecticut, no other New England urban center, with the exception of Boston, has so imposing a skyline — a tight cluster of tall buildings rising photogenically along the shores of the Connecticut River. At this writing, Hartford (population 160,000) has more buildings 300 feet or more in height than either Phoenix or San Diego (population approximately 1,000,000 each). If you like the soaring symmetry of clustered urban towers, Hartford won't disappoint you.

At Constitution Mall, a slightly elevated downtown complex of office buildings with walkways, lawns, ramps, pedestrian overpasses, and so on, you can ramble about in comfort and get excellent photo coverage of tall buildings and various architectural features. For shots of the entire skyline, by far the best bet is that often-criticized through-the-windshield view, as you cross the river from the east on the big interstate highway bridge (I-84, merged with other routes). Come across here at sunset, with a red sky in the background and the lights coming on in a dozen tall buildings, and you've got a terrific shot potential. The city is close in front of you, the bridge parts, and traffic in the foreground adds life and action.

You can of course find your way to the levee just opposite downtown for some photographic views but until they sensibly create at least a small park over there, it will require some exploring, both with car and on foot — don't be surprised if you have to cross

No other New England urban center, with the exception of Boston, has so imposing a skyline.

THE CONGREGATIONAL CHURCH IN OLD LYME WITH ITS TOWER DESIGNED BY CHRISTOPHER WREN.

railroad freight sidings, climb a chain link fence or two, and perhaps be chased by an armed guard.

Hartford's state capital area, with its adjacent Bushnell Park and various grand edifices, seems almost to have been designed for photographers. The capitol building itself, a large, traditional domed structure with interesting gothic-Victorian touches, is always a good subject, and with plenty of open spaces around it, extremely easy to photograph well. There is much opportunity here to photograph a state capitol (or any public building) the way such buildings *should* be photographed — not head-on, or even at an unobstructed slight angle, but with something else in the foreground, be it a reaching tree branch, collonade, arch, garden, or the edge of another structure.

Elsewhere in the Connecticut Valley, there are a number of scattered landmarks that you might not wish to go miles out of your way to photograph, but that are worth pointing a camera at if you're in their vicinity. These include historic Wethersfield, immediately south of downtown Hartford on Route 99, with its 1752 Joseph Webb House and other edifices of the past; East Granby, on Route 20 north of the Hartford area, with a Revolutionary War prison and nearby old mill; and Gillette's famous castle at Hadlyme, on Route 82, 20 miles north of Norwich — a 24-room structure with an oddly cakelike fieldstone facing. There is also Mark Twain's balconied home in West Hartford, immediately adjoining Hartford on Route 4, and if you're traveling southwest from Hartford on I-84, check out the architecturally striking clock tower at Waterbury, an emulation of Renaissance Italy.

Check out the architecturally striking clock tower at Waterbury, an emulation of Renaissance Italy.

Northern Connecticut

NORTH OF A LINE drawn east-west across Connecticut through Hartford, the state quite abruptly shifts its pattern from frequent urban to predominantly rural. Immediately north of the fast-growing city of Danbury, where I-84 and Route 7 intersect, the woodlands of the upper Housatonic valley contain much natural beauty. Candlewood Lake, 10 miles long, has long been a vacation resort, though without a busy tourist center or showy resort complexes. Bordered by forest and low hills, it provides a boating and swimming retreat for many Connecticut residents and New York City summer escapees. It is most easily reached by taking Route 37, then Route 39, north from I-84 at Danbury.

The Housatonic River is itself photogenic, especially from New Milford northward. There are attractive bends with heavily wooded hills on each side. Highway 7 follows it fairly closely and affords a number of scenic views. A few miles east of the river, at the little village of Washington, the American Indian Archaeological Institute offers a reconstructed Indian village that can easily whet your picture-taking appetite.

Litchfield, 15 miles east of Route 7 on Route 202,

THE HOUSATONIC RIVER.   has one of those classic village greens, complete with another tall, admired Congregational church tower. Power and telephone cables have long frustrated photographers attempting to capture this church on film. The late Clarence Chamberlain, painstaking dean of New England black-and-white architectural photography, solved the problem by carefully re-touching every one of those lines out of existence on his large negative.

The state's upper right quadrant is surprisingly thin in population, but has rural communities here and there with an intriguing air of orderly tranquility about them. Here a fine old homestead; there a tree-lined lane; and beyond them an old stone brook crossing. There is much here for what used to be called "camera club" photo creativity. this is roughly the region between I-84 and I-395 and north of the Hartford-to-Providence Route 6.

At Greenwich, in the southwest corner of Connecticut, speeding along on Interstate 95, you will unceremoniously leave New England. No executive director's name will appear in the sky to indicate the close of your visit — just the gradual appearance of impersonal blocks of high-rise apartment communities. Returning New Yorkers may feel a pang at the realization that their vacations have ended; those from father away may feel only concern at facing traffic-filled parkways and complex bridges before they can continue on course. But whatever category you may be in, we hope your camera bag will be now be filled with worthwhile exposures.

THE CONNECTICUT STATE CAPITOL IN HARTFORD.